Thanks to To[illegible] .

No sh[illegible]

No sola[illegible] snow.

No warmth, [illegible]mfort or bright cheer

In heav'n above or earth below.

from 'Trench Winter. November 1916' by Noel Clark

Jigsaw

Chaos theory . . . Events that seem random always have a reason for happening, even if we don't understand it at the time. For instance, a black car passes a cyclist on a rainy evening. A boy dies. The connection?

Annie has always been an outsider in her English school. Uprooted from her home in Norway when her parents split up, she has never felt accepted by her peers; and one of her chief tormenters is Grant Penney, always the first to tease her about her 'Viking ancestors' and her 'funny accent'. But when Grant commits suicide, Annie feels compelled to try to find out what had driven such an outwardly confident and brash person to such despair. As the pieces of the jigsaw finally fall into place, Annie is forced to realize that maybe she and Grant had more in common than she thought.

Carol Hedges was born in Hertfordshire and after university, where she gained a BA(Hons) in English Literature, she trained as a children's librarian. She has had various jobs including running her own children's clothes business, being a secretary, a dinner lady, and a classroom assistant at a special needs school. Later she retrained as an English and Media teacher and worked in a large comprehensive school. In 1999 she gave up full time work to concentrate on her writing. She has had four books published and a short story broadcast on the radio. *Jigsaw* is her first novel for Oxford University Press.

Jigsaw

Carol Hedges

OXFORD
UNIVERSITY PRESS

OXFORD
UNIVERSITY PRESS

Great Clarendon Street, Oxford OX2 6DP

Oxford University Press is a department of the University of Oxford. It furthers the University's objective of excellence in research, scholarship, and education by publishing worldwide in

Oxford New York
Athens Auckland Bangkok Bogotá Buenos Aires Cape Town Chennai Dar es Salaam Delhi Florence Hong Kong Istanbul Karachi Kolkata Kuala Lumpur Madrid Melbourne Mexico City Mumbai Nairobi Paris São Paulo Shanghai Singapore Taipei Tokyo Toronto Warsaw

and associated companies in Berlin Ibadan

Oxford is a registered trade mark of Oxford University Press in the UK and in certain other countries

First published 2001
First published in this paperback edition 2002

Database right Oxford University Press (maker)

British Library Cataloguing in Publication Data available

ISBN 0 19 275171 9

1 3 5 7 9 10 8 6 4 2

Typeset by AFS Image Setters Ltd, Glasgow

Printed and bound in Great Britain by
Cox & Wyman Ltd, Reading, Berkshire

■ I was fifteen when Grant Penney committed suicide

My name is Agnetha—Annie for short. My surname is Skjaerstad, it's Norwegian. I'm five foot six, light brown hair which I wear up or tied back because it gets greasy, blue eyes, fair skin. I don't like my face—my cheeks are too flat and my mouth is too big. And I could lose a stone in weight but it's hard. Especially in winter. My mother says it is part of the Norwegian temperament to eat in the winter, so that's my excuse. I have no excuse for the rest of the year.

The Tuesday Grant died started just like any other day. The alarm went off at six-thirty. I swore and tried to ignore it. My mother shouted up the stairs. I swore and tried to ignore her. Finally got up, showered, had breakfast (cold meat, cheese, bread, jam.) I got dressed, looked for my homework, couldn't find it, swore a bit more and finally left the house at eight. I cycle to school. It takes me twenty minutes.

I parked my bike in the cycle shed and then hung around outside B block until the bell went at eight forty-five. Registration with Mr Richards followed by Citizenship. During the Citizenship lesson, we discussed our work experience choices. Many of the girls wanted to work with young children or in a shop. Not me. I wanted to be a detective or maybe a crime writer when I finished college. That was my dream back then. So I asked to work with the police. I thought I might get some useful inside info on how they deal with crime. Ironic, as things turned out. But of course, I didn't know that.

Citizenship was followed by French. Then break. I bought an iced bun (brain food) and went looking for someone interesting to talk to. Didn't find anybody. After break, double Art. Then lunch. I had a pizza, chips, and an apple—I always try to have something healthy every day.

After lunch I walked round with Helen Hogan and Tracie Simpson. I don't have any real close friends. I hang out with anybody who's doing interesting stuff.

Today, we talked about work experience and whether we should get paid for it. We agreed that we should. Helen, who had asked to work in a legal practice because she wants to be a lawyer, was really cross.

'I could be dealing with real cases,' she said. 'So I deserve a real salary.'

'The whole deal stinks,' Tracie said. 'The clothes shop people get staff discounts and all sorts of perks.'

'Do they?' I didn't know this.

'Oh yeah,' she went on. 'My sister Donna worked in Clothes-4-U last year and she got first pick of the new spring collection.'

So that explained why so many girls had chosen clothes shops.

'That's not fair,' Helen said. She liked things to be fair.

'Tell me about it.'

It started to rain, so we went in and hung around outside the Drama Studio where the only warm radiator is.

'Why do boys play football in the rain?' Tracie shuddered.

'Because they are animals,' I said. 'They don't care like we do.'

'They're all nerds,' Helen said. 'Name me one decent boy in our year.'

'Lee Scott?' Tracie suggested.

We thought about Lee Scott.

'OK, *apart* from Lee,' Helen said.

'Simon Farrow?' Tracie suggested.

I felt a boring boy-fest coming on.

'OK, I have to get to the library before registration,' I said. 'Catch you later.'

I checked some books out of the library and then went back to my form room via the toilet which was full of Year Nine girls having major hair and nail traumas.

After registration, my favourite lesson: double English with Mrs Taylor. I have a lot of respect for Mrs Taylor. I don't give her the hard time I give other teachers. Even when I arrive fashionably late, she is cool about it.

'Good afternoon, Miss Skjaerstad,' she says, without looking up from the register. She is the only person in the school to call me by my surname and she pronounces it correctly too. That's why I give her respect.

I went and sat at my desk, back row by the window. Outside, it was still pouring with rain. Small spitty droplets were even coming in through a gap in the window frame. I felt depressed. My life is like rain, I thought, very grey, very boring. Nothing interesting ever happens. I sighed.

'Open your poetry anthologies,' Mrs Taylor said, shutting the register and standing up. 'Page 75, please. We're going to look at some of the poems written during the First World War.'

I opened up the dog-eared book and read:

'Trench Winter, November 1916' by Private Noel Clark (1898–1917).

There was a black and white photo next to the title. Young man with thin moustache, wearing a soldier's tin hat.

Listlessly, I started to read the poem:

No shelter from the kniving wind
   No solace from the driving snow.
No warmth, no comfort or bright cheer
   In heav'n above or earth below.

It was good. Despite my gloomy mood, I read some more:

My soul longs to be far from here,
   To be with those who care for me.
   Far from the noise of conflict grim
Where lives are toss'd on Death's dark sea.

I glanced at the photo again and this time, I noticed something interesting. The man's mouth was smiling but his eyes had a sad, faraway expression. I did a swift bit of mental maths—nineteen, I thought. Bloody hell, he was only nineteen when he died. And I thought I had problems! Suddenly, I felt better. Unexpectedly, I'd found something to relate to.

After school, I worked in the library for a bit. Then I went to get my bike. The wintry rain was coming down even harder as I cycled out of the school gate. I turned my collar up and wished I had brought my ski-hat. I had to keep blinking the rain out of my eyes.

Then, suddenly, without any warning, a big black car passed so close to me that I nearly lost my balance. I wobbled and swore loudly. The driver hooted a couple of times. A passenger in the front seat, who looked vaguely familiar, waved mockingly at me out of the back window. I hate it when people do that, so I raised two fingers. The car drove off at high speed.

I got home cold, wet, and starving. I needed food and TLC. Instead, I found a note: *Soup in pan. Sort out washing. Back late, don't wait up. Tusen takk*, I thought—thanks a lot!

I went upstairs and threw my bag across the room. Got changed. Then I returned to the kitchen and set about creating a gourmet supper for myself. I heated the soup (vegetable) and fried up as much bacon as I could find. There is nothing more warming on a cold miserable day than hot soup and bacon sarnies! I added some yogurt and a banana. I carried my loaded tray upstairs and put some good music on.

I worked steadily through my homework. Finally, at ten-thirty, my brain declared time-out. I closed up my books, set my alarm for six-thirty, and got ready for bed.

Just another ordinary day. But it wasn't. Because sometime that evening, Grant Penney made a noose out of his bedsheets and hanged himself in his bedroom.

■ Norwegians love telling stories

It passes the long, cold winter nights. We even have special names for the tales: Eddas and Sagas. These stories are always about gods, battles, kings, and heroes. When I was a child, I remember my grandfather in Oslo telling me tales of the Viking gods and heroes: Odin, Thor, and Eirik Bloodaxe.

'What did they look like, *bestefar*?' I always asked.

'Who knows?' my grandfather would reply, smiling. 'Maybe they looked like you and me. Just ordinary. Perhaps you might pass one of them on the street and not realize he was a great hero.'

This used to amuse me. The idea that a god or hero could be quite ordinary. That you might not know who he was.

While I got ready for school, I kept thinking about Private Noel Clark, the young soldier who'd written so poignantly about life in the trenches before dying at nineteen. Had he been a hero?

As I cycled to school, I made plans. I would find out more about Private Noel Clark. I decided I'd go to the library and look through the poetry section. There must be other poems somewhere. I felt good as I turned in at the gate. My black mood of yesterday had been replaced by one of buoyant hope. I had a purpose in life. I even waved cheerfully to a group of girls from my year as I went to put my bike in the shed.

The first indication that something was wrong came at registration. The bell went; we all piled into the form room. No teacher.

'Mr Richards's overslept . . . must've had a hot date!' one of the boys joked.

We waited.

'Maybe somebody should go to the staffroom?' Helen queried. She liked things to be done properly. I could see why she wanted to be a lawyer.

We waited a bit longer.

Then people started to relax. Moved onto the tables to chat to their friends. Unwrapped gum and dropped the paper on the floor. I looked out of the window and thought: on a day like this, Private Noel Clark sat in a mud-filled trench somewhere on the Somme, writing his poems. Did he suspect that in just a short time he would be dead? Would he have written differently if he'd known?

Then the door opened. Mr Richards strode quickly into the room. His face was white and he was carrying a piece of paper. At once the chatter died away. Silence descended. People slid into their seats, exchanged puzzled looks.

'Right. Can you all listen very carefully,' Mr Richards said quietly. Normally, he was loud, jolly, liked to clown around with us. Now, he spoke softly, hesitantly. He kept glancing down at the piece of paper. 'I have to tell you all with great sadness that Grant Penney will not be coming back to school.' He paused. Looked down. 'Last night, he was found dead in his room.' Another pause. 'It appears that he took his own life.'

I remember the silence that followed his words. Nobody moved. We sat, frozen in a time warp. Unable to take in what we'd just heard.

Mr Richards cleared his throat and went on, 'Now, it is possible that we may have reporters outside the school in the next few days. I cannot stop you talking to them but I would urge you *not* to speak to anybody from the press. There will probably be lots of rumours about Grant's death going round the school. Please do not believe everything you hear, nor encourage others to do so. Above all, please respect Grant's family and the suffering that they're going through.'

He stopped. Waited. Another long silence.

Someone asked, 'How did he do it?'

Mr Richards shook his head. 'I don't know,' he said. 'I can't answer you.'

And suddenly, everyone began to speak at once. Questions . . . questions . . .

Mr Richards held up his hand and the noise died away. 'There will be a special Head's assembly for the whole school this afternoon after registration,' he said. 'Meanwhile, if anybody wants to talk or just sit quietly, the Pastoral Base will be open. There will be people there to help you. Or you can go to any of the staff.'

The bell went for first period. As if in a daze, we picked up our bags and filed out of the room in absolute silence. Nobody said a word. It was as if we were all holding our breath. I was the last to leave. I remember that very clearly because at the door I turned round. Mr Richards was slumped behind the desk, his head in his hands. He looked as if he was crying.

What can you say when somebody you know dies? For four years, ever since Year Seven, I had shared a form room with Grant, gone to the same lessons. For a short period in Year Eight, I'd had to sit next to him as a punishment. He had been part of my everyday life. I hadn't liked him much, nobody had liked him much, but he'd been there. Now, I'd never see him again.

Over the days and weeks that followed Grant's death, I, like everyone else, would experience many emotions. On that first day, however, I don't think I really felt anything. All I wanted to know was: what had gone on? I wanted answers, details.

But the details that emerged over the morning were pathetically few. Grant had been in school all day yesterday. Played football at break and lunchtime with Lee, Simon, and some other Year Eleven's. He got into trouble in Science and was threatened with an Upper School detention on Friday—nothing new. He'd gone to PE. Stayed behind for a half-hour training session. Then he'd gone home.

What happened next was speculation mixed with a few facts: Grant must have gone up to his room, probably played on his computer, mucked around. Sometime later, he'd put a tape on loud and killed himself. His mum, working the twilight shift at Tesco, had got in at 10.30. Heard the music. Realized after a while that it was a continuous loop. Went upstairs to check. Found Grant. Rang the ambulance but it was too late.

Lunchtime, I ate alone in the canteen. Everyone ate alone that day.

After lunch I didn't feel like walking round school so I made my way back to the form room. I found most people had had the same idea. We sat around in silence for a while.

Then Helen spoke.

'I heard he was being bullied,' she said. She was sitting on the window ledge, biting her lip, twisting her fingers together.

'Grant?' exclaimed one of the boys. 'Get real—who'd bully Grant?'

'I'm only saying what I heard,' Helen snapped back. Everyone was on edge, nervous, shocked.

'Who told you?' one of the girls asked.

Helen shrugged. 'I just heard it, OK,' she said sulkily.

That's how it was. On that first day, all rumours were absorbed uncritically, like stains wiped up by sponges. I'd heard that one too. Who told me? Who knows. Like I said, we desperately needed to know why Grant had died. So we made up our own reasons. Better than nothing. Because nothing was all we had to go on. Soon, it would be different.

'Babe trouble,' one of the boys said. 'It was babe trouble.'

'Yeah—which babe?' someone asked.

'I heard he was trying to get off with Carly Spencer in 9M.'

An explosion of laughter from the rest of the boys.

'You don't go and top yourself because you can't pull a girl,' someone scoffed.

'Carly Spencer? Geez, I'd bloody top myself if I *did* pull her!' Lee said.

Lee Scott really annoyed me. He was tall, with dark floppy hair and brown eyes. He was good looking and popular and he played on it. Flirting with the female teachers. Getting girls to fetch and carry for him. He was Grant's friend though none of us understood why. They were complete opposites. Grant was short, stocky, liked causing trouble and winding people up. I didn't think Lee should be making jokes, acting like nothing much had happened. I stared at him coldly.

'That is a sexist remark!' I said. Lee looked at me. Then he turned to his mates and pulled a face.

'Whoa—Viking alert . . . Viking alert!' he intoned. The boys laughed.

'And *that*'s racist!' I said icily.

'Touch-ee,' Lee drawled.

I swore at him.

'Furr—cough yourself!' he sneered, imitating my accent. More laughter.

I turned my back on him. *My soul longs to be far from here* . . . the sad words of Noel Clark's poem drifted into my mind.

The Head's assembly was a straight re-run of Mr Richards's talk. Word for word. Same script, bigger audience. Once again we were warned against speaking to the press. Told not to believe all the rumours (too late). Invited to talk to someone if we felt the need. Then a minute's silence out of respect for Grant and his family, which was strangely moving.

We filed out of the hall. Everybody was very quiet. It was beginning to sink in what'd happened. Then it was last lesson. Wednesday, we always finished early after period four. Not that we'd learned much that day. Or been taught much. The teachers were all in shock too. I'd seen several in tears as the day went on. It made me feel strange. Teachers don't cry.

I didn't feel like hanging around to chat after school so I went straight to the cycle shed. On the way, I found a Mars bar in my bag. My favourite comfort food. In the cycle shed, I found Lee Scott. Not my favourite person. He was looking a bit upset. About time, I thought.

'Getting your bike?' he said.

'No, I'm playing the bloody violin,' I told him coldly. I hadn't forgotten what he'd said. Nor forgiven him. Lee and Grant. They'd both liked teasing me. Now there was only Lee.

'You know what gets me,' Lee said, ignoring my put-down. 'I was probably the last person to see Grant alive.' He frowned. 'We were getting our bikes after footy training. I said, "See you tomorrow."'

'Right,' I said, unlocking my bike. I wasn't particularly listening.

'See you tomorrow,' Lee repeated slowly. 'And now he's dead. Makes you think, Viking, doesn't it?'

That night I lay in bed wondering just how Grant had killed himself: Pills? Razorblade? I'd tried a razorblade. The summer my grandfather died. Just stroked it across my wrist to see what it felt like. A pain to take away the pain. I remember sitting on my bed, sun pouring through the open window, watching the beads of blood forming. Scary. I'll never do it again: I had to wear long sleeves for weeks.

There is always something worth living for. Only losers gave up on life. Grant Penney was a loser. I felt sorry for him. That was all. He had the charisma of a road accident. Nobody liked him. Or so I thought.

So it was somewhat of a shock to me when I got to school next day and walked right into a grief-fest. It was weird. I wandered into my form room to discover practically the whole class in tears. It was as if they'd just lost their best friend in the whole wide world. Even sensible people like Helen were sobbing away. I felt like reminding her about when Grant had found the box of Tampax in her bag. Or the time he'd deliberately put a bag of cold greasy chips in between the pages of her History project.

There were things to cry about—the futility of war, the death of young poets. These were worthwhile. Grant Penney was not in the same league. Trouble was, as the day wore on, I seemed to be the only one who thought this. People kept breaking down and having to be sent to the Pastoral Base for counselling. It was illogical. How could they have forgotten what Grant was really like so soon? I decided to ask Helen about this during Biology. We were sitting next to each other on the back bench.

'Why are you so upset?' I whispered to her. 'You never liked him.' As soon as I'd opened my mouth, I realized I'd made a terrible mistake.

Helen glared at me. Her eyes were puffy and red-rimmed.

'How can you say that?' she hissed. 'Grant was my friend.' And she laid her head down on the desk and started sobbing loudly.

Miss Mitchell, the Biology teacher, moved swiftly to Helen's side and put a comforting arm round her heaving shoulders.

'Now, now, Helen,' she soothed. 'Come on, you must be strong.'

'It's her.' Helen's voice was muffled by Miss Mitchell's white lab coat. 'She's saying nasty things about Grant.'

'What? I never did!' I exclaimed indignantly, but it was too late. Everyone stopped their work and turned round. Twenty-five pairs of accusing eyes bored into me like machine-gun fire. Oh shit! I thought.

'Annie.' Miss Mitchell's voice was cold and hard. 'I think you should apologize.'

'What for?' I said stiffly. I hate conflict.

'I think you know very well what for,' Miss Mitchell continued, tight-lipped. She didn't like me.

'I never said anything,' I repeated, feeling bits of me closing up inside. The whole class continued to give me evils.

'I'm waiting,' Miss Mitchell said.

'I'm not apologizing for something I didn't say,' I said, forcing the words out.

There was a long silence.

Miss Mitchell started breathing very hard. 'Annie,' she said. 'Perhaps you would like to go and see the counsellor?'

'No,' I replied, 'I wouldn't.'

Miss Mitchell's face was an iron mask. 'I think you had better go and see the counsellor,' she said, icily.

'Why?' I asked.

At which point, Miss Mitchell lost it. Little flecks of spit started gathering at the corners of her mouth. 'You'll go because I tell you to!' she shouted at me, her face bright red. 'Now, pack your bag and get out of my lesson!'

You could have cut the atmosphere with a knife. I stuffed my books into my bag and got up. As I walked to the door, head held high, making no eye-contact with anybody, a low hissing started up. I stumbled out into the corridor and slammed the door shut behind me.

It was ten past eleven, too early for lunch. Not that I was feeling hungry. One thing was for sure: I wasn't going to see the counsellor. If anybody needed help, I thought indignantly, it certainly wasn't me! I set off down the corridor and, almost without thinking, pushed open the double glass doors that led to the outside world at the back of the school. There was a little path that crossed the playing fields. It led to a thicket of trees at the far end of the school grounds. Technically, the area was out of bounds, but everybody knew it was where the smokers hung out. I decided to make for the thicket and nurse my wounded pride for a bit.

I pushed my way in between the bushes and crouched down. Feeling in one of my pockets, I found some gum and unwrapped it. It felt strange to be there on my own in the middle of the day. Everybody else was in lessons. I didn't care. They could all go to hell as far as I was concerned. I slid into a more comfortable position, trying to avoid sitting on any of the millions of ciggie butts that littered the ground like discarded confetti. That was when I saw it. Out of the corner of my eye. Something silver, glinting on the ground, under a bush. I crept forwards and parted the foliage. It was a bike. A silver mountain bike. Very expensive. A top of the range machine. I looked at it and felt myself going cold all over. I knew who owned that bike: Grant Penney.

Of course I should have gone straight back into school and reported what I'd found. That was the sensible thing. Unfortunately, I wasn't in a sensible frame of mind, so I did exactly what I shouldn't have done: I panicked. I scrambled to my feet, picked up my bag and ran back across the playing field into school. I got my coat. Jammed my ski hat on my head. Then I went straight to the bike shed, grabbed my bike and cycled as fast as I could out of the gate. I didn't stop until I got home.

Bunking. Everyone did it. I did it, but not often which was why I never got caught. I would have got away with it this time too, except that there was a local film crew lurking outside. I didn't see them. They saw me though. I found that out later, when the local news came on TV. There was a report on traffic problems in the area. The usual: people moaning about the number of cars pulling up outside school. Sixth formers driving too fast. Kids crossing without looking left or right. It happened all the time. Reporter on pavement. Old lady who'd lived there 200 years wittering on about young people today. Close up on her face, mid-shot of the school with reporter standing in front of it. Then, a long shot of the school driveway with a lone cyclist pedalling like mad towards the camera. A lone female cyclist wearing a navy coat and a black and white ski hat. Hot damn!

■ Maybe God doesn't like me

There has to be a reason why bad things happen to me. I remember having this discussion with an RE teacher in Year Nine. The meaning of suffering. Why some people always get away with stuff while others, like me, get dumped on all the time. She tried to explain it. Something to do with free will, but I wasn't convinced. Perhaps that's why I don't get such good grades in RE. In Maths and Geography, you have answers: right or wrong. No maybe's . . .

I was thinking these profound thoughts as I waited outside the Head's office next morning. It was amazing how many people had watched the early evening news. I had lots of comments. The comments varied from, 'Hey, I saw you on TV last night' to a hand drawn silently and dramatically across the throat.

It's hard to read our Headmaster. Sometimes he can be very nice—if you win a cup or do something good for the school. Other times, watch out. He also does the most boring assemblies on the planet. I suddenly remembered, as I stood waiting for the summons, how Grant used to try to disrupt them by farting loudly. Maybe I should remind Helen and the rest of them about those assemblies too, I thought, as the door opened and I went in.

'Sit down.' The Head pointed to a chair. I sat and waited for the thunder clouds to break over my head. I knew I was in deep trouble. Bunking is taken very seriously. I was anticipating at least a day's suspension. Possibly a phone call to my mother's place of work.

'How are you getting on?' The Head always started like this. The Spanish Inquisition technique, lull the victim into a sense of false security, before the blow falls.

'All right, sir,' I said cautiously.

'Having a difficult time, eh?'

I waited politely. Hard to react until I knew what line he was going to take.

'Year Eleven? You've got your mocks coming up soon, haven't you?'

I nodded, still waiting for some clue as to what he was about.

'And then there's all the sad business about Grant.'

Aha! Now I could see where this was leading. I looked down at the carpet and sighed deeply.

'Finding it all a bit hard to come to terms with, eh?'

'Yes, sir,' I said in a small voice, still keeping my head down. I fumbled in my pocket for a non-existent handkerchief and breathed a silent thankyou to the Drama teacher.

'You know there are always people around to talk to.'

'Yes, sir.'

'No need to go running off like that.'

'No, sir. I won't do it again.'

'No, I'm sure you won't. I'm sure you're a sensible girl . . . Agnes.'

Agnes? I looked up. The Head was frowning at a piece of paper on his desk. Somebody had obviously written my name on it. Illegibly.

'Right . . . ' he glanced down at his watch, 'Agnes, is there anything else you wish to tell me?'

Funny how important decisions can hinge on such little things. If he'd not looked at his watch, if he'd really known who I was, maybe I would have told him about finding Grant's bike in the woods . . . but as it was, I just shook my head.

'Right then. Off you go.'

'Thank you, sir.'

At lunchtime, I went to the library to research Private Noel Clark. The library was proving to be a bolthole for me as most of my class were ignoring me. They had gone into injured silence mode: I had broken the unwritten taboo—speaking ill of the dead. I was glad it was Friday. Maybe things would be calmer next week.

I searched through all the World War I poetry books on the library shelf; there were so many poets and they all seemed to have died tragically young. A few of the books had pictures—graphic paintings of No Man's Land or wounded soldiers being carried from the battlefield. It was all so very sad, and so unnecessary. Finally, I found one book that had a couple of poems by Private Noel Clark—'Trench Winter', the poem we were studying in class, and another poem, 'Survivors'. They appeared to be the only two poems he'd published. I checked the book out at the issue desk and then returned to my classroom. Nobody looked up or greeted me as I went in. Nobody walked with me to lessons. The only person who spoke to me was Lee Scott. Just as we were leaving to go home at 3.40.

'Nice one, Viking,' he hissed.

I went to get my bike, hating all of them.

I had heard politicians on the TV talk about a 'war of words'. Suddenly I felt as if I was in a war as well—a war of silence.

■ I'm a heroine addict

One of my top heroines is Freyja, Norse goddess of beauty. Freyja led an army of Valkyries—female warriors. They were strong, powerful, and lived in a place called Valhalla, where they fought and feasted. Every now and then, the Valkyries went down to earth, collected a few dead heroes and brought them back to Valhalla to join in the party.

I admit it, some of the appeal is definitely the feasting. But I like the idea of being strong. I've grown up with the concept. It's in my bones and my blood. When my father left, my mother told me to be strong. Strong people survive, she said. They don't go under. Same when my grandfather died: weep but be strong. Strong people don't show their feelings, don't talk about them. That's how I am.

That evening, I opened up the book of war poetry and found Noel Clark's poem 'Survivors'—an auspicious title, I thought.

We lay all night out under the stars.
No noise of battle to disturb our rest
Only the quiet pacing of the moon
As she looked down upon our resting place.
We lived. Survived another day,
All fears forgotten now, we craved
Only sleep and blest dreams of home.
And when dawn's pale fingers touched our faces,
We awoke, stretched cold limbs
And waited for the call to 'come and dine.'
A piece of bread and jam, a mug of milkless tea,
No banquet, yet it tasted sweet to me.

The consolation of poetry—Mrs Taylor had mentioned it recently but I hadn't understood. Now I knew exactly what she meant. This was the second time Noel Clark's poetry had spoken to me, given me hope. If he could endure to the bitter end, I thought to myself, then so could I.

I spent the weekend creating a sort of shrine to Noel Clark—I'd mentally dropped the 'Private'—it was too impersonal for the way I felt. I photocopied the poems, blew up the grainy photo and stuck them to the wall above my desk.

So they would be the first thing I'd see every morning when I woke up: the two inspirational poems and Noel Clark's hauntingly sad face and dark brooding eyes. The notes at the back of the book explained that he had been in the 13th Royal Fusiliers and had died at the Battle of Arras in 1917. 159,000 British soldiers had died in that battle, which had been fought in a snowstorm. Many of the troops had no shelters, but were forced to sleep out in the snow, in the biting cold winter wind. It made the poems almost unbearably poignant to read. I could scarcely imagine what their lives had been like, the suffering they'd endured. 200,000 German soldiers had died as well.

Good guys, bad guys

My mother was nineteen when she met my father. She was visiting Norway on a skiing holiday, he was a history teacher from Oslo, taking time off to teach skiing to foreign tourists. Holiday romance. A year later, they married and moved in with my grandparents. A wooden house with red-tiled roof, polished beech floor, and painted wooden cupboards. In summer, we all packed up and went to the coast, to the family *hytte*—the holiday cottage. I remember it well, swimming in the icy blue lake under a clear sky, picking berries, walking in the clean-smelling pine forests. Then, when I was ten, my father decided to make a trip to Finnmark. He was writing a book about the history of the Stone Age people and wanted to examine the rock carvings at Hjemmeluft, which are over 2,000 years old.

So he went north, to the mountains and the fjords and the snow, where the winter temperature can drop to −50 degrees and the sun never sets from May to the end of July. And he never came back. My mother had a letter from him saying that he'd decided to go and live with the Sami people—the nomadic reindeer herders. He wanted to research their culture. The Sami have their own traditions and hundreds of different words for snow. I guess my father probably knows them all by now. Twice a year, Christmas and birthday, I get a card.

Chaos theory. A butterfly beats its wings in China, a tidal wave hits the west coast of America. The unconnected connect. I believe in it. Events that seem random always have a reason for happening, even if we don't understand it at the time. For instance, a black car passes a cyclist on a rainy evening. A boy dies. The connection? Maybe a reindeer in the far North stamped its hoof.

By Monday morning, the news of Grant's suicide had reached the press. There were journalists at the school gate. I took no notice. I was still bruised from my last encounter with the media. I didn't see anybody from the upper school talking to them either, but as I cycled past, I saw some lower school kids being interviewed. Not good news. Their imagination and their mouths work in direct proportion to their brains.

I went into my form room, head held high. I wasn't going to give them the satisfaction of seeing I cared. I needn't have bothered. Nobody was interested in me. Everyone was gathered round Lee Scott's desk. He and Simon had been round Grant's house over the weekend.

Now at last, there were some details. Apparently, Grant had hanged himself in the bedroom he shared with one of his small brothers. 'He would've died sitting down,' Lee said. I don't know why, but that made it somehow worse. Lee also told us that both Grant's brothers were away at a sleep-over. 'He'd never have done it if they'd been there,' he continued. The police had been round, but were not going to investigate it. They were carrying out a post-mortem examination. There would be an inquest, but there were no 'suspicious circumstances'. No? Completely out of the blue, a fifteen-year-old boy hangs himself and it isn't suspicious? What was with these guys? I thought disgustedly.

Simon said that Grant hadn't left a letter, nothing to

explain why he'd done it. The police had suggested to his mum that he might have been mucking about and it had somehow gone wrong. Especially since the tape he'd been listening to when he died was by a band whose lead singer had also died by hanging himself in the bedroom of his apartment. So to all intents and purposes, Grant Penney had died in a copy-cat suicide attempt. Another example of the typical 'stupid easily-influenced teenager who can't think for himself' syndrome. End of story. It made me really angry. Why do adults think we are all mindless robots—offer us drugs and we take them, press a button saying 'die' and we obligingly kill ourselves. It isn't like that. Except that, angry as I was, I had to admit it was just the sort of crazy stunt Grant would try.

At registration, Mr Richards told us Grant's funeral was going to take place on Wednesday. The Head would attend on behalf of the school. Helen went round with a card, which we all signed. Then we went to our classes. Now we knew why Grant had died. It had been a tragic accident. We felt relieved. Except for me. I seemed to be the only one who had unanswered questions. Like why had Grant's brand new bike been dumped in the woods at the back of school? But I didn't share this with anybody because there was no point. I knew I'd only get slagged off again. So I said nothing. I kept my mouth shut.

I also kept my mouth shut when, later on that day, some kids found Grant's bike in the woods and took it round to his mum's house. Since I've been at this school, I've become an expert in the art of self-preservation. Definition of self-preservation: hang around on the outskirts. Say nothing. Wait.

■ My mother hung around in Oslo and waited for my father to come back

After a year, even she realized that he wasn't going to. So

she packed up and returned to England, taking me with her. She found a small flat and enrolled me in the local comprehensive.

I still vividly remember that first day at my new English secondary school. I'd been looking forward to it for ages. In my school in Oslo, we loved it when new kids came into the classroom, especially if they were from another country. We enjoyed finding out about them and their life. In my 11-year-old innocence, I assumed it would be the same in England. I remember standing at the front of the class whilst the teacher called for silence. I remember her saying: 'This is Agnetha,' and I smiled. Proud of who I was.

Nobody smiled back.

'Agnetha comes from Norway,' the teacher continued. I waited for the 'interested' noises. Silence.

'Does anybody know anything about Norway?' she went on. More silence. Then:

'They're total crap in the Eurovision Song Contest,' a boy at the back called out.

Everybody laughed and I felt myself turning bright red with shock and embarrassment.

'That's not funny, Grant,' the teacher rebuked the boy. 'Norway is a very fascinating country with a lot of history. You've all heard of the Vikings, haven't you? Well, they came from Norway.'

That was the beginning of it. From then on, Grant and his friends always greeted me with: 'Sing us a song, Viking!'

For a week, I cried bitterly and begged my mother to return to Norway. Then, slowly, I began to adapt. I learned to ignore the gibes and taunting. I stopped trying to shake hands with everyone in the morning as I'd done in my other school. I spat out my gum on the floor, not in the bin. I tried my level best to fit in. But I never did. It was an impossible task, like trying to hide an elephant on an ice-floe. Whatever I did, underneath, I was still me. I knew it. They knew it too.

On Tuesday, the local paper came out. There was an article about Grant splashed all over the front page under a big banner headline: Local Pupils mourn Popular Teenage Suicide. It was enlightening reading. I'd never realized Grant Penney was so popular, so intelligent. The journo who wrote that article was a genius. He could have made Jack the Ripper out to be a public benefactor. There were even some quotes from a couple of Year Sevens about how Grant had helped them settle in. That was interesting too. I remembered Grant and his mates liked to hang around the third floor of the Lower School Block and gob on the new kids. Perhaps that was what they were referring to.

However, the article went on to make some disturbing allegations. There were hints about bullying. Suggestions that undetected stress may have played some part in Grant's death. Oblique references to drug pushers seen outside the school. In other words, the usual misinformed crap that meant somebody from Sensation Seekers Anonymous (lower school branch) had been shooting off their mouths. Great, I thought. Just what we all needed. Especially after my appearance on TV. Whenever the school gets a bad press, we get a hard time. Now nobody would trust us for weeks.

Wednesday, the day of Grant's funeral, it rained. Curdled grey clouds blew across the sky. Everyone was subdued at school. I guess we were all feeling sad, imagining the line of black cars snaking slowly along the road towards the cemetery. Grant's mum and his two younger brothers standing in the rain looking at the funeral wreaths laid against the wall. Wet flowers shedding their bright petals on the soggy grass. Dead leaves blowing in the wind.

After lunch, we all hung around our form room. The mood could best be summed up as sombre. I sat at my desk, keeping my head down and quietly reading my poetry book. It seemed an appropriate thing to do.

'Well,' one of the boys said, glancing at his watch, 'it'll be over by now.'

'Yeah,' Tracie sighed. She and Helen had begged Mr Richards to let us all take the day off to go to the funeral. Mr Richards had said no. It was to be a family affair, he said. Very small, very private. Helen and Tracie had been quite upset by this. Now that Grant was dead, they'd taken on the role of chief mourners and took their duties very seriously.

'I think it must have been an accident like the police said,' one of the girls remarked. 'Like in Year Eight when he did that thing with the hamster and the belljar.'

People nodded, murmured agreement. I kept on reading. I remembered Year Eight. In my opinion, Grant had suffocated that hamster on purpose. I recalled the look of glee on his face as the poor animal rushed round its glass prison, fighting desperately for air before collapsing in a little furry heap. Then the door opened and Lee came in. He threw his bag across the room and swore loudly. Everyone looked up, shocked.

'Hey, chill,' Simon said.

'No, I won't chill,' Lee snapped. 'You read the graffiti in the boys' toilets?'

'No. What's it say?'

'Grant Penney was a smackhead. Big letters.'

'It's lower school kids. Just ignore it.'

'Yeah—but where'd they get the idea from? That flaming article in the paper. I'm going to kill that bloody journo.'

'Look, it doesn't matter.' David put out a hand. Lee shook him off.

'Journos always write crap. Everyone knows that. Nobody believes it,' Simon added.

'Yeah, like that stress thing,' Tracie put in quickly. 'Everyone knows Grant never got stressed.'

'He was only doing four subjects, wasn't he?' one of the boys said. 'I thought he'd been kicked out of most classes.'

'PE, English, Science, and Maths, eh, Lee?' David asked, trying to draw Lee back into the group.

'Not sure about Science,' Lee replied, frowning. 'He hadn't done any of the coursework. Miss Mitchell's been having a cow about it.'

'Miss Mitchell is a cow,' David said. It was not much of a joke but everyone laughed, eager to break the tension.

'She doesn't like you, does she, Viking?' Lee said slyly, glancing quickly across the room.

I looked up from my book. Was this the beginning of another 'get-Annie' session?

'So?' I said evenly.

'Just saying. So what you reading then?'

I felt the muscles round my jaw tightening. Why couldn't he let me be?

'Some poems.'

'Yeah . . . poems is it?'

'Oh leave her alone, Lee, for God's sake,' Helen snapped.

Lee stared at her, his mouth falling open in astonishment. I knew just how he felt—I couldn't remember anybody ever sticking up for me either. Ever since I'd arrived, I'd always fought my own battles.

'Oh? Since when have you two been mates?' Lee said. 'I thought you were the one who said she was—'

'Look,' Helen cut in swiftly, 'Grant's dead, OK. We shouldn't be fighting. It's . . . ' she searched for the word, 'it's dishonouring.'

'Yeah,' Tracie agreed, in her role as second mourner-in-chief, 'we should show respect.'

'Oh yeah?' Lee turned to face her, 'and what respect are you showing then? You don't know anything.'

'OK, mate,' Simon spoke quietly, 'take it easy.' He put a hand on Lee's shoulder but Lee shrugged him off.

'You act like you're sorry now but you all hated him, didn't you,' he went on, angrily. 'Well, let me put you and everyone else straight on a few things, OK? Grant wasn't stressed. He wasn't being bullied and he wasn't doing drugs. Got that?' He glared round.

'Come on, mate,' David said, 'we're all gutted.'

'He never did drugs,' Lee went on, ignoring him. 'He had respect for himself, right? Like all the training he did—he was always working out. He kept himself in shape. You couldn't do drugs and be as fit as Grant was.'

'It's OK,' one of the boys said.

'No, it's not,' Lee interrupted. 'It's not bloody OK.'

We all stared at him. Lee Scott, cool, confident, was suddenly, unexpectedly, coming apart in front of our eyes. Lee stared back at us, eyes like a caged animal. Then he grabbed his bag and ran out of the room, slamming the door behind him.

There was a long, shocked silence.

'Well . . . ' Helen said at last, primly.

'Poor Lee,' Tracie breathed staring at the door.

'He's been on a knife edge for days.' David shook his head. 'Blames himself. Says he should have known what Grant was up to.'

'But how could he?' Tracie said.

David sighed. 'I told him that,' he replied. 'I said, you never know what's going on in somebody's head. Specially somebody like Grant.' He got up. 'I'll go and talk to him.'

Lee Scott wasn't in class that afternoon. From where I sat in the Humanities block, I could see him. He was walking round and round the games field, on his own, in the rain. Once, the teacher went over to the window and looked down at him. Then he turned away without a word. If I hadn't disliked Lee so much, I might have felt sorry for him. But I didn't. Four years of hurt can't be washed away just like that. And I don't forgive easily.

■ Anger is a cruel master

When my parents split up, I was angry. I blamed everybody: my mum, my dad. Most of all, I blamed myself. If only I'd been prettier, cuter, I reasoned. If I'd worked harder at school. If I'd been someone different, maybe my mum and dad would have stayed together for me. I was full of anger. Anger and worthlessness.

Then when we got to England and I realized I was never going back to Norway, I was angrier still. I could not believe my dad would abandon me in this strange, alien place. I found it hard to forgive my mum for taking me away from my own country.

I was angry with the kids in my new school. Especially Grant Penney and Lee Scott, the two boys who had laughed at me on my first day. Grant and Lee, with their silly jokes about Abba and Vikings. (They were so stupid they couldn't even tell the difference between Sweden and Norway!) Almost every day they said or did something—called me names, hid my stuff, mimicked my accent. Everyone laughed. Nobody told them to stop and I was too scared of worse happening to go tell a teacher. So I put up with it. Suffered in silence.

That's all I remember about my first years in England—a red haze of anger and pain, with me in the middle, struggling to make sense of it. Sometimes I think I'm still struggling.

I got an A for my essay on the War poets. Mrs Taylor read it out to the whole class.

'Well done, Annie,' she said. 'Terrific empathy.'

It was easy to feel empathy. Every morning when I woke up, the first thing I saw was Noel Clark's sad face. Each time I sat at my desk to work, I read the haunting words he wrote. I was beginning to feel I knew him personally. That, somehow, we were linked. I cared more about him than about Grant's stupid suicide or Lee's anger or any of the others still trying to cope with their emotions. I had no empathy at all for what they were suffering. I didn't even think it was suffering. Not then.

On Friday, Mr Richards handed out our work experience envelopes. It was the first good thing to happen for two weeks. Relief from the grief. Everyone ripped open their envelope to see if they'd got their placement choice.

'Yeah! SuperSports.' David punched the air with his fist.

'Hey, I got Frocks 'n' Rocks.'

'Little Ark Playgroup—brill!'

I opened my envelope: Elmfield Nursing Home, I read.

What?

Bewildered, I stared at the piece of paper.

'Mr Richards.' I raised my hand.

'Yes, Annie—is there a problem?'

'Yeah,' I said, 'I think I got the wrong placement.'

'Let me have a look.'

I walked to the front of the room and handed him the piece of paper. Mr Richards checked it against his list.

'No,' he said, 'there's no mistake. It's quite right.'

'But . . . ' I stuttered, 'I asked for the police.'

'Sorry, Annie,' he said, 'we can't all get our first choice.'

'Yeah, but this wasn't anywhere on my choice list,' I protested.

'Well, there are always some disappointments, but it's only for a week.'

'Can't I go someplace else?'

There was a pause. Mr Richards sighed. 'Annie,' he said, 'it's been a very difficult time for all of us. I'd really appreciate your co-operation. Can you do that for me?'

God, I hate it when teachers give you the guilt trip thing.

'Yes, sir,' I said, picking up the piece of paper like it was poisoned. 'OK, I suppose.'

'There's a good girl,' Mr Richards said, like I was a little kid. 'And there are lots of your friends working nearby.' He glanced down at the list. 'Helen's at a law practice just down the street. You could meet up after work.'

'Great,' I muttered. Helen gets what she wanted. I don't. I stumbled back to my seat, trying not to show I cared that I was the only one in the class who hadn't got somewhere good to go to.

'It might be very interesting,' Mr Richards called after me.

Sure.

'What did you get?' one of the girls asked, as I sat down.

'None of your frigging business,' I replied, stuffing the piece of paper into my bag.

'Suit yourself.' She shrugged, turning her back on me.

At break, I went to see the Head of Year. Not to complain, just to check. After all, there could have been a mistake further up the line which Mr Richards might not know about.

Actually, quite a few other people seemed to have the same idea. There was a queue outside her office. It reminded me of Marks and Spencer after Christmas—everyone returning unwanted gifts of cardigans and socks. By the time I got to the front of the line, the bell was about to go and Mrs Allsop was fresh out of sympathy.

'Don't tell me—you want to change your work placement,' she sighed.

'It's just that I asked for something completely different,' I said, trying to sound reasonable.

'Yes, maybe you did. You and the other twenty-five Year Elevens.'

'So can I swap?'

Mrs Allsop looked at my piece of, by now, very crumpled paper.

'Well, Annie, I've got one spare placement.'

'Yeah?' I asked.

'The Cybercafé—interested?'

'What's that?'

'It's one of those computer places, where people go to get on the Internet or do business.'

'I'm not very good with computers,' I admitted. Slight understatement. I can wipe off files like there's no tomorrow.

'That doesn't matter, you won't be on your own. There's another student on that placement.'

'Who?'

'Lee Scott—do you know him? He's quite a computer expert.'

I stood and thought about this. A week with Lee Scott and a lot of computers which I couldn't work and he could. I'd heard people say humiliation is character building.

'Well?' Mrs Allsop said impatiently. 'Make up your mind, the bell's going in two seconds.'

I sighed and picked up my piece of paper. 'I'll take the nursing home,' I said.

Depression hits in different ways

Some people (the thin lucky ones) go right off their food. I eat. So when I got in after school, I made myself a massive plateful of high calorie goodies and went up to my room to pig out.

'It isn't fair,' I told the picture of Noel Clark. I'd somehow got into the habit of telling him the personal stuff that I couldn't share with anybody else. He listened. That was the big difference. Also, he didn't laugh, call me names, or, like my mother, say he was too busy. So I sat stuffing my face and having a really good moan. Later, feeling much better (and fuller) I got up, brushed the crumbs from my desk and went to ring the nursing home. We'd all been told by Mr Richards to ring our placements and introduce ourselves.

'Hi,' I said, cautiously, 'I'm Annie.'

The woman at the other end sounded OK. She told me her name was Mrs Morrison and she was matron at the home.

'We're looking forward to meeting you on Monday,' she said.

'Yeah?'

'Oh yes. The old people love seeing a new face, especially if it's a youngster.'

'Umm . . . great.' I tried to sound equally enthusiastic.

'There's lots for you to do.'

'Err . . . good.'

'You'll be in the kitchen helping the catering staff to start with. Then we'll see how you get on. I think you'll have a very busy time.'

'Sure.'

'I'm so pleased you chose us. So many young people today don't have time for the elderly. It's a refreshing change to meet somebody like you, Annie.'

Groan.

'Ah . . . yeah, right.'

'So we'll see you on Monday morning at nine o'clock? I'll meet you at reception in the foyer.'

'I'm really looking forward to it,' I lied.

I've never got used to the cold here. I think I've been colder in England than in Norway. It's not the temperature so much as the wind and the rain. I remember that first English winter, the rain slapping me round the face like a wet towel as I cycled to school. I hated the clammy dampness of the air. I never felt dry and warm. I had more colds that first winter than in all the rest of my life put together. '*Jeg er allergisk mot England*,' I told my grandfather. It was not a joke. Every week, I phoned 'home' to speak to him. To hear his voice, to have a conversation in my own language. To ask whether my father had come back. As if.

The day my grandfather died, I was on my own in the house. It was Saturday. My mother had gone to London to meet somebody. The phone rang early in the morning. Half-asleep, I stumbled downstairs.

'*Ja?*' I always lapsed into Norwegian when I was dozy.

'*Er dat fru Skjaerstad?*'

'*Ja.*' Not too intelligent either.

And because she believed I really was my mother, the nurse told me. How my grandfather had slipped on the ice whilst crossing a busy road to the shops. How the oncoming tram couldn't avoid him. It had been a peaceful end, she said—no suffering. Just a quiet drift from unconsciousness into oblivion. No pain. She was sure about that. No pain at all.

I remember sitting on the stairs, not crying, remembering. Little things—the tobacco smell of his pullover. Old hands gently carrying a little cat that had strayed into the garden. One of his home-made cakes on a blue china plate. And I thought that now I'd never go back to live in Norway, because they would sell the house. That door had slammed shut on me.

Later, I went upstairs and counted out my carefully hoarded savings. Money I'd been secretly putting by for the trip back to Norway. I'd nearly saved enough. I had it all planned—my things in my rucksack, taxi to the station, train to Newcastle, then the ferry to Stavanger. I looked older than thirteen, nobody would question me. It's easy to run away, you attach yourself to a family, pretend your mother is just a bit behind you in the queue. But of course I didn't see it as running away. In my mind, I was returning. Now, there was no point. I had nowhere to return to. So I took the money and bought food and candles. To celebrate his life. Like the Viking warriors of old, I sent him on his final journey with feasting and joy.

Somehow, the news about my grandfather's death reached my father because he was at the funeral. First time I'd seen him for three years. I hoped maybe my parents might decide to get back together again. United in sorrow. Or maybe they might do it for my sake, but they didn't. Happy endings are only for story books. My father returned to the far north. My mother and I came back to damp foggy Britain. The house in Oslo was sold.

Monday morning blues

The first day of my work experience and it was a grey, drizzly day again. Apparently global climate change is caused by people leaving their computers on sleep instead of switching them off. I read that in the paper, as I sat in reception at Elmfield Nursing Home, waiting for Mrs Morrison. Not my fault then, I thought to myself: I don't have a computer.

I'd never been inside a nursing home before—I'd always visualized them like on *The Simpsons*—gloomy, depressing places with a notice saying: Thankyou for not talking about the outside world. Elmfield Nursing Home was a bit of a culture shock—pale peach walls, thick carpet, and a selection of the day's newspapers on the counter. It was almost like the foyer of a hotel, except for the smell. Hotel foyers smelt of expensive room freshener. This place smelled of stale cooked food and weak disinfectant. I recognized it. Like school. The institutional smell.

As I followed Mrs Morrison, I was aware of curious eyes watching my progress across what the brass plaque on the door called the 'Residents' Lounge'. Elderly people huddled in chairs peered up at me as I passed. Grotesque dolls. In one corner of the lounge, a TV blared out the usual morning rubbish. Nobody seemed interested.

'Right then, Annie,' Mrs Morrison said, pushing open the swing door next to the hatch. 'This is Mrs Jones, and this is Mr Reeve.'

Two middle-aged people in maroon overalls looked up from buttering bread and smiled politely.

'I suggest you get on with washing up the breakfast things,' Mrs Morrison said, 'then we'll see, shall we.' And she turned briskly on her heel and walked off, leaving me in a kitchen with two complete strangers and a sink full of sticky porridge bowls and jammy plates.

Great, I thought, rolling up the sleeves of my jumper. A whole week of washing up. How much worse could it get?

I went over to the sink and turned on the hot tap. A jet of scalding water shot out, spraying me in the face. I jumped backwards, bumping into Mr Reeve.

'Now then, young lady!' Mr Reeve was tall and thin with a face like an elderly basset-hound. 'You need some Marigolds, don't you?'

'What?'

'Have we got any Marigolds in the drawer, Sue? Small ones, I think.'

He's crazy, I thought. Why do I need flowers to wash up? Mrs Jones, who was plump and grey haired, opened a drawer in the work-table and produced a packet of pink rubber gloves.

'Got some, Malcolm.'

Mr Reeve took them and solemnly handed them over as if he was presenting me with an award.

'Got to wear your Marigolds.'

'Er . . . right.' The packet had 'Marigold gloves' on it. OK, I thought. A week of washing up with two refugees from a geriatric TV sitcom. Got it. I put on the gloves, feeling like a brain-surgeon, and returned to the sink.

I washed up. The kitchen became hot and steamy. A radio played oldie music in the background. Mrs Jones and Mr Reeve made sandwiches and talked about what they'd done over the weekend. I tried not to listen, which wasn't difficult, as they'd done nothing interesting. Mr Reeve had put up a shelf. Mrs Jones had planted bulbs in a tub. Her grandkids had visited on Sunday. Made a change from the usual Monday gossip, though. These two definitely weren't into parties, drink, or sex. After a while, my mind switched off. My body got into a rhythm. My hands moved automatically, dunking plates, rinsing, stacking. Actually, it was quite soothing. And, I reminded myself, at least it wasn't school.

'Tea?'

I jumped. I was so deep in my own thoughts, I'd almost lost contact with the real world. Mrs Jones was standing next to me holding a mug. She smiled.

'Yeah, OK,' I said.

'You're a hard worker, aren't you? Milk, sugar?'

'Milk, two sugars, thanks.'

She set the mug down on the draining board.

'You can stop for a break now.'

'OK. Great.'

I peeled off the gloves and wiped my forehead with the back of my hand. I felt boiling. I drank some of my tea and glanced at the clock on the wall. Five to ten. If this was a normal Monday, I'd be in French. Colouring the pictures in my text-book. Waiting for the break bell. Hoping all the iced buns hadn't gone before I got to the canteen.

'I like a nice cup of tea,' Mr Reeve said. 'How about you, Annie?'

'Yeah, great,' I said.

'Got to have tea, haven't you,' Mr Reeve added. He was drinking his tea from a flowered cup.

'Can't beat it.' Mrs Jones sighed, sipping.

'No,' I said. I'd never had a conversation about tea before.

'Are you from one of the local schools?' Mr Reeve asked, replacing the cup carefully onto its saucer.

'Yeah,' I said. Any minute now, I thought, one of them is going to say something about school being the happiest days of your life.

'Happiest days of your life, school,' Mr Reeve said. He

selected a biscuit from one of the plates on the hatch and nibbled it.

'I don't suppose she thinks that, Malcolm.' Mrs Jones laughed.

'It's OK,' I lied.

'You make the best of it, love,' Mrs Jones said, placing her empty mug in the sink. 'Time flies so quick, you'll end up in a place like this before you know it.'

'Like us, eh,' Mr Reeve said. This time they both laughed.

I finished my tea and returned to the washing up. I felt Mrs Morrison should have warned me about the kitchen staff. They looked normal, but they were definitely on the far side of reality. By mid-morning, I'd done more washing up than in my whole life. I'd mopped the floor, wiped down all the surfaces and decided to give a career in catering a miss.

'Right then, Annie,' Mrs Jones said when I'd finally run out of areas to clean, 'one more little job and then we'll start laying up for lunch.' She handed me a bowl of crusts. 'Nip out the back and give these to the birds, will you?'

I took the bowl and carried it towards the swing doors. I almost expected to see a notice: Danger, you are now leaving Planet Kitchen and entering the real world. Outside, it had stopped raining. I carried my bowl round the back of the nursing home to the garden, enclosed on all sides by a high brick wall. There was a terrace with benches for the old people to sit on. The garden looked a bit sad—bare flowerbeds and soggy grass but I guessed it was lovely in the summer. Nice for the oldies to have somewhere peaceful to go, I thought. I stood on the edge of the terrace and began tearing up the crusts and chucking them on the soggy lawn.

I didn't notice the old man at first. He was so still that he almost seemed part of the garden. Then something, some movement, made me look up and I saw him. A small, bent, little old man, standing under one of the bare-branched trees. His hands hung lifelessly by his sides and he was staring at me. His deeply lidded eyes held no expression in them. There was something weird about him. He just stood absolutely still without moving in the dying autumn garden. The breeze lifted his few strands of pale hair but nothing else about him moved. His tweed jacket was too big and his corduroy trousers fell over his shoes, as if his clothes had been bought for somebody much larger.

I was really spooked—how long had he stood watching me? I tried a smile, followed by a cautious wave, but there was no reaction. The man continued to stare, his face unmoving. All at once, I felt scared, a cold shiver went down my spine—no normal person could remain so motionless for so long. For what seemed like ages, we stared at each other. Then, suddenly, the man stood to attention and saluted. I screamed, dropped the bowl and ran.

'Are you all right, Annie?' Mrs Jones asked as I burst into the kitchen.

'Looks as if she's seen a ghost,' Mr Reeve added.

'Come and sit down.' Mrs Jones pulled out a wooden stool and patted it invitingly.

I collapsed onto it, hot and panting. My heart was pounding in my chest.

'I saw a weird old man,' I gasped. 'In the garden. He stared at me.'

I saw them exchange puzzled looks.

'He stared at me.' I knew I wasn't making sense. 'It was like he was there, but he wasn't at the same time.' I struggled to put my feelings into words, 'I think . . . the garden might be . . . haunted.'

'Haunted?' Mrs Jones frowned. 'Never heard that one before and I've worked here for three years. What do you think, Malcolm?'

'A ghostly old man in the garden,' Mr Reeve said, thoughtfully, 'I wonder . . . ' He went to the door and flung it open.

'Hello?' he called. 'Anybody there?'

There was a silence. Then we all heard the sound of shuffling footsteps. Almost frozen with fear, I stared at the open door. The footsteps came nearer and nearer. Suddenly, they stopped. I looked and my mouth fell open. Framed in the doorway was the old man I'd seen in the garden. He was carrying the bowl. Silently, he held it out to me.

Mr Reeve turned to me and said, 'Is this your "ghost"?'

I nodded, too scared to speak. My heart was pounding in my chest.

Mr Reeve took the bowl. 'There now, Billy,' he scolded. 'You frightened Annie.'

The old man hadn't taken his eyes from my face. Once again, he slowly brought his hand up to his forehead in another salute. Then he turned and shuffled slowly away.

'Why did he do that?' I asked shakily when the footsteps had died away.

'I guess he thinks you're a soldier,' Mrs Jones said. 'Must be your clothes.'

I looked down. I was wearing my camouflage trousers, a khaki-coloured jumper, and workboots. 'Got a fixation with the army then, has he?' I muttered. I felt a bit embarrassed—clearly I'd overreacted.

'You could call it that, I suppose,' Mrs Jones said. She loaded the plates of sandwiches onto a trolley. 'You see, Annie, time stopped for Billy eighty years ago. On a battlefield somewhere in France.'

The past throws a long shadow

Billy Donne was 18 when the call came to 'go over the top'. It was July 1, 1916. At 9.00 a.m., the company sergeant-major shouted: 'Over the top, but don't run,' and he went, together with 100,000 other young men. It was the first day of the Battle of the Somme. The soldiers had been told it would be a walkover. By the end of the day, 60,000 of them lay dead or wounded. Billy survived.

Mrs Jones told me the story as we set the places for lunch in the dining room.

'He's a walking miracle,' she said, whisking knives and plates neatly onto the tables.

I did a bit of swift maths: 'He must be really old.'

'Over 100. I was here for his hundredth birthday. Lovely do it was. Message from the Queen, big party. Malcolm—Mr Reeve—made him a beautiful cake. It was all in the papers; Mrs M.'s got an album full of photos and cuttings in her office.'

I continued putting glasses and jugs of water on the tables. Life and death were such random events: one soldier died, another survived; there was no logical reason why. I struggled to make sense of it.

'There's not many of them left now,' Mrs Jones went on. 'Still, I don't suppose you're interested are you? Pop music and clothes more your scene, eh!'

It really annoys me when people stereotype me.

'Actually, I'm very interested,' I said stiffly. 'We do World War I poetry as part of our GCSE.' Up yours, lady! I added under my breath.

Mrs Jones wheeled the cutlery trolley back to the hatch.

'Oh well, you should look at the album, then,' she said tartly over her shoulder.

Yeah, I thought. I reckon I might just do that.

I didn't see Billy again that day. He wasn't in to lunch. He was so old and frail that he was allowed to eat his meals in his room. So I passed round plates of sandwiches, poured drinks, and said my name, very loudly, to all the oldies. After everybody had eaten their lunch, I collected the plates and loaded them onto the trolley. I passed round cups of tea and told the oldies my name once more as nobody seemed to have remembered it. They didn't have big attention spans in Elmfield, but they were very friendly. I mopped, cleaned, and smiled. Then I helped some of the less mobile residents back to their rooms before returning to the kitchen. There were a lot of leftovers from lunch piled on the counter—two plates of untouched tiny crustless sandwiches and some chocolate biscuits too.

'Pity to see it all go to waste,' Mr Reeve said, surveying the sandwiches sadly. 'They don't eat a lot, but we still like to make it nice. They need a bit of coaxing.'

I felt a sudden unexpected wave of gratitude towards the oldies. I never needed coaxing.

'You don't have to waste it,' I said, 'I'm happy to help out.'

I polished off all the little sandwiches, drank another mug of sweet tea, and said a silent farewell to my dreams of a flat stomach and thighs of steel. Then I tidied the residents' lounge and laid up for supper. Maybe this wasn't the work placement of my dreams, I thought, but it was OK. Better than school. The most strenuous mental activity I'd done all day was tell people my name. There was plenty of food. A mysterious old man living in a World War I time warp. I was almost singing as I returned to the washing up.

When I got home after work, my mother was in. She'd prepared a nice meal. Guilt trip. I'd been fending for myself for the past fortnight whilst she'd been working. I don't mind though, we're not close—I'm too Norwegian, she's too English. I told her a bit about my day—not much—as far as most adults go, I subscribe to the mushroom principle: keep them in the dark and feed them shit! I never used to be like that. But then I used to have people I was close to: my father and grandfather. Ironic. The people I'm close to, I never see any more.

So I ate the meal and pretended to play happy family for

a bit. Then I went upstairs. At 9.30 the phone rang. It was Tracie. I was genuinely shocked—I hadn't expected anybody to ring me. And guilty, I hadn't intended to ring anybody myself.

'How you getting on then?' Tracie asked.

'Oh, OK, you know,' I said. 'How's the playgroup?'

'Messy,' Tracie said. 'I can't understand a word they say and they get covered with dinner.'

'Yeah, know what you mean,' I agreed. 'My lot are a bit like that.'

'Helen's enjoying her placement,' Tracie continued. 'She's going to court tomorrow.'

Yippee for Helen, I thought. I expect she'd be wearing her brand new £200 business suit that we all heard so much about.

'That's nice,' I said non-committally.

'She likes you really,' Tracie said. 'Don't let that stuff she said get to you. She was upset.'

'Yeah, right.' And I wasn't?

'She stood up to Lee for you, didn't she?' Tracie reminded me.

'That was so kind of her,' I said. I didn't mean it to sound sarky. Honest.

There was a pause at the other end of the phone. We said a few more things but the friendliness had gone. Then Tracie rang off. I went back to my room. I don't know why I get so prickly. Maybe it's the way people speak to me. As if they were doing me a massive favour. Like being Norwegian meant having a communicable disease. Don't get too close to Annie, you might catch something nasty.

I wondered why Tracie had phoned. It wasn't something she'd ever done before. Then I remembered Mr Richards saying sometime in the week, we should all try to ring the person next on the register. To keep in touch. Simpson, Skjaerstad. That explained the call. She wasn't being friendly, merely obeying orders. That also meant I was supposed to ring Anthony Unwin. Tough. I wasn't going to. It was only later I suddenly remembered that neither of us had mentioned Grant. Strange. The Grant-shaped hole left by his absence was filling up so quickly. As if we'd come to accept his death and moved on. Except for Lee. He was the only one who still cared. I closed my eyes and tried to recall what Grant looked like. And found I could scarcely remember him at all. His image was fading so fast, like an old black and white photograph.

Billy Donne survived the war, but he did not survive the peace. In 1918, the war finally ended. The guns fell silent at the eleventh hour on the eleventh day of the eleventh month. It was called an Armistice. Thousands of men had died—but thousands lived who might just as well have died. Their minds were shattered by what they had experienced. They were shell-shocked or gassed. Mutilated beyond recognition, they wandered around the silent battlefields unable to come to terms with what had happened. Billy Donne was one of those. His country, that he had believed in and fought for did not know what to do with him. No family claimed him. Nobody wanted him. So he was put in a mental asylum and left to rot. He was only twenty years old.

When I arrived at Elmfield on Tuesday, Mr Reeve was in the kitchen on his own. The sink was full of washing up. I said hello politely. I had the feeling Mr Reeve liked polite people. I got the Marigolds from the drawer and ran the hot water.

'What are you making?' I asked, interested. Food always interests me.

'Fairy cakes.'

It sounded good. I hoped there would be plenty of leftovers.

'The elderly like a nice fairy,' Mr Reeve added, ladling runny yellow batter into some bun tins.

There are times when I wish I didn't have such a vivid imagination. I suddenly got a mental picture of the Elmfield oldies all chomping on fairies—the tiny wings and bent wands hanging out of their mouths. It was so disgustingly awful that I had to pretend I'd got washing up liquid up my nose.

'Sue says she's been telling you Billy's story,' Mr Reeve went on, ignoring my spluttering noises at the sink.

'Yeah.' I fished around for some teaspoons.

'She said you knew all about First World War poetry.'

'We read some at school.'

'Got any favourites?'

'I like Wilfred Owen,' I said.

' "Dulce et Decorum est . . . for something-something" . . . can't quite remember it,' Mr Reeve intoned.

' "Pro patria mori". Yeah, it's good, that one. And I like Noel Clark.'

'Can't say I recall him.'

'He didn't write many poems. He was killed when he was nineteen.'

'Well, so many of them were, weren't they. Terrible times.'

'I think war is obscene,' I said bluntly.

Mr Reeve carried the tins over to the oven. 'I always wear my poppy,' he said rather complacently. 'Put 50p in the tin. Do my bit to remember our glorious dead.'

But it wasn't glorious, I thought. It wasn't dulce et decorum . . . a sweet and decorous thing. It was ugly and cruel and wrong. Millions of men died needlessly. Wilfred Owen was killed four days before the Armistice; Noel Clark, with his suffering face and his haunted eyes, died before he had even begun to live. And Billy? Locked away in a lunatic asylum for seventy-five years. As good as dead.

Yesterday, I'd been scared of Billy Donne. A ghostly old man standing alone in a winter garden. Now, I wanted to see him again. I wanted to take a good look at somebody who'd been alive at the same time as the poets I'd studied, who'd maybe shared the same experiences. Had he lain out all night under the stars? Tasted pure happiness in a mug of tea or witnessed the harrowing sight of a comrade slowly dying of gas poisoning?

Whilst I was thinking this, Mrs Jones arrived in the kitchen and told me I could go and look at Billy Donne's album after work. 'Mrs M.'s really pleased you're taking an interest in poor Billy,' she said. 'He never gets any visitors. A forgotten hero, that's what he is.'

I finished the washing up and had my mug of tea. Then I picked up the bowl of crusts and went out into the garden alone.

At first I didn't see him. Dressed in faded earth-tone colours, he seemed to blend with the trees and shrubs, becoming part of the natural world. I scattered bread on the grass and a few bold blackbirds swooped down immediately and began to feast. Then I spotted him. Out of the corner of my eye. No sound. He just seemed to emerge from nowhere.

'Hello, Billy,' I said softly.

We stood, some distance apart, watching each other and the birds as they devoured their bread. Now I noticed how his skin seemed stretched tight across his eggshell-thin skull. I saw the brown age-spots on his forehead, his wrinkled, pitted cheeks. He was certainly the ugliest person I'd ever seen—a cross between the Hunchback of Notre Dame and a garden gnome. It was hard to imagine he'd once been young, maybe handsome, like Noel Clark. But I couldn't look away, however repulsed I was by his appearance. For a long time we stood silently waiting until the last crumbs had been eaten.

'I have to go now,' I said. 'Bye, Billy.'

I lifted my hand and waved to him. Silently, he raised his arm and gave me his shaky salute as I went back into the house. When I turned and looked out of the french doors, Billy was standing in exactly the same spot, staring straight ahead, dead leaves blowing round his slippered feet. An old man nearing the end of his life and a garden settling into the long sleep of winter. They were made for each other.

'I saw Billy again,' I said when I returned to the kitchen.

Mrs Jones smiled. 'He's always out there, rain or shine. He loves being in that garden, watching the birds, whatever the time of year. It's the highlight of his life.'

'Doesn't he do anything—go out, like the others?'

'No,' Mr Reeve said. 'Never. He's been so long in institutions that he wouldn't be able to cope with the outside world.'

'Is he . . . happy?' I asked. It seemed such a minimal life. More of an existence.

Mrs Jones thought for a bit, her head on one side. 'I think so,' she said finally. 'He just potters around the place.'

'And he's got his drawings,' Mr Reeve added.

'Drawings?'

'Oh yes, he's a bit of an artist.' Mr Reeve nodded. 'Battlefields, that's what he draws mainly. And soldiers. That's how they knew he'd been in the war.'

'But he doesn't talk about it?'

Mrs Jones shook her head. 'He never says a word. Come to think of it, I don't think I've ever heard him speak—have you, Malcolm?'

'He doesn't say a lot—I don't think he's spoken more than a couple of words to me in the years he's been here.' Mr Reeve piped pink icing onto the cakes. My mouth was watering. 'Mind you, if you imagine what he's been through in his life, I reckon he must think he's in Paradise.'

When Billy Donne was 95, the asylum that had been his home for so long was closed. Times had changed. People didn't like to think of mentally ill people being locked away. Care in the community was the buzzword. So the patients were rehoused. Not Billy, though. Nobody knew what to do with him. He'd spent so long in the lunatic asylum that the reason he was put there in the first place had got lost in the mists of time. The doctors who treated him had left the asylum ages ago. His records were mislaid or destroyed. The only facts known about him were his name and his date of birth. And the drawings. He was obviously incapable of living independently, so it was decided to put him into Elmfield Nursing Home, where he could be looked after properly.

After I'd finished work, I went to Mrs Morrison's office. I stood outside the door, feeling guilty. I always feel guilty whenever I stand outside doors. I reckon it's a school thing. Miss Mitchell, my biology teacher, would probably say I should get counselling for it.

'Come in, Annie.' Mrs Morrison looked up from behind her desk. I almost went into my 'Sorry, I really didn't mean to do it' routine but stopped myself just in time.

'Sit down.'

I lowered myself into one of the comfortable chairs. The walls were painted a soft peach colour. There were flowery curtains at the window. On her desk was a bowl of early hyacinths, gently scenting the air with their sweet perfume. The room had a soothing, peaceful atmosphere. I guessed maybe this was the place they brought people to hear that their elderly relatives had taken a turn for the worse or had died. It had that sort of feeling.

'How are you getting on?'

'Fine,' I said, cautiously.

'The kitchen staff tell me you're working hard—that will look good on your report, won't it?'

'Yeah, thanks.' I'd forgotten each placement had to report back to school.

'And I gather you're interested in our Billy.'

I nodded.

'That's great, Annie. As you've probably gathered, Billy has had so few people in his life.' Mrs Morrison opened a drawer in her desk and took out a square, green-backed photo album. She leaned across and handed it to me.

'Perhaps you'd like to look at this. It's Billy's scrapbook. To remember his special day.'

I opened the album. There was a photo of Billy next to a news report headlined: **'A happy 100th for man with mysterious past.'** I read the article and looked at the photos on the following pages: Billy with his birthday cake, Billy with the mayor, Billy with the staff, Billy with the local MP, his message of congratulations from the Queen and a selection of birthday cards. I noticed that in all the photos, Billy was looking away from the camera with a faintly puzzled expression on his face. Poor old guy, I thought. Bet he hadn't a clue what the hell was going on.

'He's a very special person,' Mrs Morrison said.

'Yeah, I can see that.'

'I think it's such a shame when old people are just abandoned by their families,' Mrs Morrison continued.

It was an innocent remark, but her words suddenly cut me like a knife. I remembered my grandfather. Maybe he'd thought we'd all abandoned him. Perhaps he'd lain there dying in that hospital bed, wanting his family. I'd pushed the terrible thought away from me for a long time. Now, the pain came flooding back like an unhealed wound. Tears filled my eyes and I fixed my gaze upon the white hyacinths.

'I'm sure Billy will appreciate your taking an interest,'

Mrs Morrison went on. 'I know he doesn't say a lot, but everything goes in, believe me.'

'Yeah?' I'd got control now.

'He has his own way of communicating, if you know what I mean.'

'Maybe I could . . . visit him sometime?' The words came from somewhere. I wasn't aware I'd said them, but Mrs Morrison beamed at me like I'd just presented her with a Lottery cheque.

'Really, Annie? Would you like to? That would be wonderful. Billy would so appreciate it.' She kept on smiling. I was finding it hard to get a grip: people on the other side of desks didn't usually look so pleased with me. 'Perhaps you could pop in some weekends,' she went on, 'that's when most people visit. It wouldn't have to be every weekend, and you needn't stay for long—ten, fifteen minutes, Billy tires so easily. How about it? Would you like to be his visitor?'

I was drowning in a tidal wave of approval. 'Yeah,' I heard myself agree. 'I might do that.'

Cycling home through the foggy dusk, I decided that I must have gone into a guiltfest—being around old people had stirred up memories of my own grandfather. Subconsciously, I'd chosen to visit Billy as a personal atonement for not being there for *bestefar* at the end. Still, I reminded myself, Billy was interesting and it would look good on my Record of Achievement. I decided I'd run it by Mr Richards next week. Even though 'next week' seemed a century away.

Over the next few days, I slipped into a routine: every morning, I worked, ate too much, worked some more and went home. It was a dreamworld. Slightly unreal. At the back of my mind, I knew time was running out. Reality was lurking just around the corner ready to grab me. I just hadn't anticipated it happening in quite such a dramatic way.

Friday was my last day of work experience. Mr Reeve was putting the finishing touches to some mouth-watering sausage rolls when I arrived at Elmfield. By now, I knew the routine. I got my rubber gloves from the drawer, put on the spare overall and started washing up the breakfast things.

'Last day with us, then?' Mr Reeve remarked, demonstrating his amazing talent for stating the obvious.

'Yeah.'

'Though it's not altogether goodbye,' Mr Reeve said, 'more *au revoir*, as they say in France.'

I hadn't a clue what he was going on about so I nodded.

'I was just saying to Annie,' Mr Reeve remarked to Mrs Jones, 'it's not goodbye, it's *au revoir*.'

'That's right.' Mrs Jones started sorting clean cutlery into the cutlery tray. 'Mrs M. says you're coming back to see our Billy.' I nodded. 'Well, I think that's lovely, Annie. Don't you think that's nice, Malcolm?'

Mr Reeve went into chin-fondling mode, a prelude to one of his Observations On Life.

'Very commendable, Sue. Not that it surprises me.'

'No?' I said. It had surprised me.

'You're a good girl, Annie,' Mr Reeve continued. 'And I said the same to Sue only the other day.'

'You did, Malcolm.'

'I'll be honest, when Mrs M. told us we'd got a teenager coming for a week, I remember telling Sue, "We'll have our work cut out for us there".'

'That's exactly what you said, Malcolm.'

'I mean, you read these stories in the press, don't you—teenagers fighting and beating each other up. I said to Sue, "We'll have to keep an eye on the kitchen knives".'

I decided to keep stumm. Once Mr Reeve got going, it was best to leave him to rant until his clockwork ran down.

'And then there's all those drugs. I said to Sue, "I'm not having any of that in my kitchen, thank you very much!" '

I had a vision of myself as a drug-crazed, knife-wielding maniac. It had possibilities.

'But fair's fair, and I have to say, Annie, meeting you has changed my mind about young people.'

'Er . . . that's great,' I ventured cautiously.

'Yes, if they're all as hard working and willing as you, there's hope for the future, that's what I think.'

'Umm . . . thanks.' I wasn't sure how to respond to this. I felt good, but guilty at the same time. After all, I'd mentally made fun of them all week.

'And it's nice to see someone enjoying their food,' Mrs Jones interjected. 'We get so tired of having to throw it away.'

'That's right.' Mr Reeve's clockwork was still ticking. 'We even have a little joke about you—don't we?'

'Yeah?' I couldn't wait to hear this!

'I say to Sue, "Our Annie certainly hasn't got Annie-rexia!" ' They both looked at me and burst out laughing. 'Annie-rexia,' Mr Reeve repeated. 'Do you get it?'

'Yeah—funnee.' I slapped a big jolly smile onto my face. 'I don't know how you come up with them, Mr R.' I glanced into the sink. There was a big black-handled kitchen knife at the bottom. God, it was tempting!

I finished the washing up, reminding myself that it was the last time. The last time I would lay the tables in the dining room. The last time. The finality of the words made me feel solemn, and a little sad. The last time.

The worst moment of the day came at lunch. I had to listen to Mrs Morrison making a little speech saying how much they'd appreciated my help. Mr Reeve and Mrs Jones stood behind the serving hatch, clapping enthusiastically. The oldies who'd got me sorted nodded and grinned gummily. The rest looked totally mystified. I busied myself collecting cups and tried to look as if I didn't care that I was going. I was surprised how sad I felt. Anyway, I told myself, I'd be back on Sunday to visit Billy. I'd told him. He hadn't reacted, but I could see from his eyes he'd understood.

The very old have a way of looking at you. It's a look that cuts straight through to what you have in common. That was the invisible thread that drew me to Billy Donne. Like me, he knew what it was like to be alone, to be in exile. And yet he was not afraid of solitude. We were travellers on the same path.

At 4.30, I said an almost fond farewell to Mr Reeve and Mrs Jones and hung up my overall for the last time. They really like me at Elmfield, I thought. At school, they didn't. Actually, this wasn't strictly true, but the thought fitted into the melancholy that had been gradually creeping over me since I woke up that morning. Like most Norwegians, I'm good at melancholy. I'm not good at saying goodbye.

I wheeled my bike round to the front and checked the lights were working. It was already getting dark. I decided to go into town. I wanted to buy Billy a present: a hyacinth bulb in a pot. He could keep it in his room and watch it flower. I wanted to get him a white hyacinth. The colour of peace.

The streetlights were just coming on as I hit the High Street. The sign over Iceland, the frozen food shop, had lost a couple of letters so that it now read: ZEN FOOD. I theorized about the yin and yang of vegetables as I dodged in and out of traffic. Then I pulled up outside the florist's. There were several trays of hyacinth and daffodil bulbs in plastic pots spilling out onto the pavement. I parked my bike by the kerb, selected a bulb, paid for it and put the brown paper cone carefully in my rucksack.

It was still too early to go home. I felt I deserved a treat—I'd been working hard all week, so I decided to cut through the alley to W. H. Smith to check out the magazines. I like *Exchange and Mart*. Especially when I can read it for free. After that, I thought I'd go to Lassiters and have a hot chocolate with marshmallows.

I wheeled my bike round the side of the florist's and down the unlit alley. I remember thinking how gloomy it was and how this time of year always reminded me of a poem we'd read in Year Nine: *No sun, no fun, November*, when a dark figure came out of a doorway and ran straight towards me. Suddenly, everything Mr Reeve had said about knives and drugs came back with vivid clarity. I froze.

The figure lurched towards me. I felt my shoulders tense as my hands went up to protect my face. My bike went crashing to the ground. I waited for the first blow to fall. When it didn't, I peered up from under my arm. And recognized my 'attacker'. It was Lee Scott. Relief mingled with fury swept over me. I scrambled to my feet and grabbed the handlebars of my bike.

'You *** ***!' I yelled at him. Then the streetlight at the end of the alleyway came on. I saw Lee's face clearly for the first time. His skin was a peculiar grey colour and there was a strange, haunted expression in his eyes. I'd never seen anybody like that before. He looked terrible. I stopped swearing. 'Lee? What's the matter?'

Lee's voice seemed to belong to somebody else. Somebody who hadn't got it under control before lending it out. 'Hello, Viking.' He struggled for a bit, his mouth opening and closing but nothing happening. 'Guess what?' he said finally, forcing the words out. 'I know why Grant killed himself.' And to my horror, I saw tears glistening on his cheeks.

■ Curiosity killed the cat

I should have walked off. Shrugged and said 'So?' Turned my back on Lee and got on with the rest of my life. But I didn't. I was curious, intrigued. So I made soothing noises. I uttered tell-me-about-it phrases and instead of going for a hot chocolate, I walked home with Lee Scott. Why? Maybe I make my own choices in life. After all, I'm not a cat.

It was going to be the best placement, Lee said. A week with proper Net-connected computers and real professionals who knew how to work them. Not the useless second rate system we had in school run by sad geeks who wouldn't recognize a high-traffic web site if it kicked them in the butt. Yeah, I went, yeah, nodding like I understood and agreed with every word. (The extent of my computer skills are: log on, type, print, log off. That's if I remember my password. Compared to me, the sad geeks are geniuses.)

It wasn't like that at first, of course. The owners of the cybercafé hadn't meant Lee to work with the clients. The first couple of days, all he did was fetch coffee, wipe tables, and look on enviously. Then, one lunchtime, he got chatting to a guy about some sports sites he'd visited. Next thing he knew, he was sitting down showing him how to access them.

The guy was really impressed and mentioned Lee to the owners. After that, he was allowed to supervise people coming in to test-drive the Net. People dropped into the cybercafé all the time, Lee said. They came to collect their e-mail, do business, or chat to people all over the world. Some people stayed all day, 'travelling'. It sounded weird to me but then I'm into technology like fish are into riding bikes.

The thing was, the backroom staff—Lee called them techies—were into a whole lot of interesting stuff. And of course, as soon as Lee'd become one of them, he was invited to stay back after work and be part of it. What sort of interesting stuff? I asked. Lee looked a bit shifty. Err . . . just stuff, he muttered evasively. Games and . . . adult stuff. If you mean what I think you mean, I told him, then you are totally pathetic, right—going to tell everyone about it when you do your Work Placement talk? OK, Lee said, fair enough, but what was I supposed to do? Shut your eyes, I said. Walk away, tell them that stuff degrades women. Lee sighed, it's not that easy. So? I said, that makes it all right?

We'd got near my street by now. I remember stopping at the corner—kids I knew from school were out on their bikes. I didn't want them to see me walking with Lee Scott. Sorry, I said, but I don't see what all this has to do with Grant. I'm getting to it, Lee said. I noticed that once again he was finding the words hard to say. It was this afternoon, he went on, slowly, I was on my own out at the back so I decided to check out . . . he came to a stop. Yeah, don't tell me, I said. I get the picture. Anyway, Lee continued, I must have keyed in the code wrong because what I got was pictures of . . . he stopped again. Yeah—pictures of what? I said impatiently. Dogs? Father Christmas? What? Kids, Lee whispered, looking away, his face twitching. I got pictures of kids. I don't understand, I frowned. Kids, Lee repeated. That's how it works. It's like an advert. An advert for what? I still didn't understand. Do I have to spell it out for you? Lee's eyes were bottomless pools of misery. The porn guys put pictures on the screen. Like mug shots. You click on one. Then they give you instructions how you can get hold of more. Now I understood. WHAT!!!! I yelled. And one of the pictures . . . Lee's voice was almost inaudible now . . . one of them . . . was Grant.

Time stood still. The world stopped turning. We stood on the street corner saying nothing. There were no words. I could hear kids in the street calling to each other. Cars going by. Dogs barking. Normal life carrying on all around us. Suddenly, I found I was shaking. A door had suddenly been opened on something dark and very evil. Finally, I whispered, 'Are you sure?' Lee nodded. You remember how he bleached the front of his hair the week before he . . . his voice tailed off, it was like that on the photo. It was Grant all right. I stared at him, Grant Penney was doing porn? I exclaimed. Lee gulped, swallowed. Nodded. You have to go to the police, I said. I can't, Lee said, I can't prove it. But you have to, I said. Yeah? he said, and what'd happen—they'd go round his house, ask questions, upset his family. So find the picture, I said. How—I told you, I used the wrong code. Work out the code, I said. Lee gave a mirthless laugh. Do you know how many codes there are? he said. We're not just talking this country, the Net's worldwide. The chances of finding it again are probably a couple of million to one. So what *are* you going to do? I asked. Find the bastards who killed him, Lee said. Then I'll go to the police. You're mad, I said, you could get into real trouble. Anyway where'd you start? Here, Lee said, Grant didn't go places; it has to be somebody local. Somebody he knew. God, you're crazy, I said. I owe him, Lee said. He was my best friend. I should have been there for him. But it was an accident, I said. No, Lee said, it was murder. Maybe he did it, but they made him. Then he looked at me. You could help. No way, I said, I'm not getting involved in something like this. Anyway, I went on, why should I? I don't owe Grant anything, nor you. It'd be better with two of us, Lee said. We could share ideas. Tough, I said. Besides, I added, even though I knew it wasn't true, how do I know you're for real? Maybe this is another of your wind ups, and I walked off. Annie, Lee called, Annie wait up. I didn't turn around.

People are like icebergs. You only see what's on the surface. Two-thirds is hidden away. Lee and Grant. I thought I knew them. I was wrong. I knew nothing. Suddenly, in a short space of time, I'd seen Lee Scott almost in tears; I'd found out that Grant had a terrible dark secret.

As soon as I got home, I went straight up to my room and locked my door. I couldn't get my head around what Lee had told me. I felt so peculiar. I'd always wondered how Grant had new clothes and stuff when his mum only worked at Tesco and he had no dad. Now I knew how. For a while I stood in the centre of the room. Then I went round picking up things, books, ornaments, holding them in my hands. I sat on my bed, cuddling my pillow. Something evil had broken into my world and I needed reassurance. Needed to feel safe.

I worked the whole of Saturday. Displacement activity. I cleaned the house from top to toe. I shopped. I ironed stuff that had hung around the ironing basket so long I didn't even remember owning it. I wrote two essays. I overdosed on normality. But I couldn't keep the thoughts at bay for ever. They kept returning, like those fears that haunt you in the middle of the night: spider-thoughts scuttling in dark corners of the mind.

I did not know what to do. I kept seeing Lee's face, the way his voice had broken as he described what he'd discovered. I remembered how he'd called me 'Annie' not Viking. I shouldn't have walked away. Cowards walk away. Now, I didn't know how to walk back, what to say. I was confused and I had nobody to confide in.

I was still undecided by Sunday, when I went to visit Billy. Elmfield was like the *Mary Celeste* at the weekend. The residents' lounge was practically empty. The weekly staff were all off. There were no cleaners, health visitors, physios, or occupational therapists bustling about. Even Mrs Morrison was away, so I had to sign the visitors' book when I arrived, as none of the weekend staff knew who I was. I had to be formally escorted to Billy's room too, like I'd never worked there.

Billy was sitting in his armchair staring out of the window. I showed him the hyacinth and put it on his chest of drawers. I'd given it a good watering the night before. The green shoot was beginning to emerge. Then we sat side by side, watching the wind blowing leaves about in the garden. We didn't speak. The good thing about being around Billy was not having to make conversation. After a while, he got up and shuffled across the room to the chest of drawers. He opened the top drawer and took out a sketch pad and an old wooden box. He returned to his chair, flipped the pad open and took a pencil out of the box and started drawing. Fascinated, I watched his bent fingers painstakingly guiding the pencil, a frown of deep concentration on his wrinkly old face. I'd never seen any of his war pictures before. Billy drew a soldier lying on the ground, badly wounded in the head. Over in the corner was another group of soldiers with their backs to him.

'That's nice, Billy,' I said encouragingly. 'Yeah, it's very good.'

Billy looked at the drawing and frowned.

'What?' I asked.

Billy raised his head. His eyes bored into mine. I struggled to understand.

'Is it something in the drawing?' I stared down at the little sketch, trying to work it out. Billy's eyes never left my face as if willing me to see what he saw. I tried to focus, to lock onto his thought patterns.

'Is it something that you saw in the war?' I asked. Billy's eyes flickered. 'Something you remember happening?' No reply. I sighed and gave up. It was too hard.

'Well, whatever,' I said, 'it's a good drawing.'

Billy held it out to me. 'Oh, right,' I said. 'You want me to have it?'

I rolled up the drawing and put it in my pocket. Billy's eyes were beginning to close. I took the pad and pencil and put them on top of the chest of drawers. Then I covered him with a rug and left him to sleep.

That evening, I pinned Billy's picture to the wall alongside my poems and my photo of Noel Clark. I wondered who the wounded soldier was and what had happened to him and whether all soldiers who fought in World War I had little pencil moustaches and mournful expressions on their faces. Whatever had happened, it had obviously made a big impression on Billy. Trouble was, I'd never get to hear the story. Still, it had taken my mind away from Grant for a bit.

Not that Billy Donne and Grant Penney had anything in common, I thought. That was like going from hero to zero.

It was hard work getting up on Monday morning with the prospect of school ahead. All my good intentions—do my coursework, sort my stuff, pack my bag the night before, had somehow failed to happen. What did happen was the usual Monday morning panic. This time made worse because my school skirt, always tight, wouldn't do up. I cursed Mr Reeve's cooking as I struggled to fasten it with a safety pin. I am not fat, I told myself, I am circumferentially challenged. But it wasn't good news. I was going to have to deal with it. I decided to skip breakfast. Inside every fat girl is a thin one, I comforted myself as I cycled to school. Yeah, my subconscious jeered, and a load of chocolate!

Monday was the first day back after work experience and everybody had a story to tell: Helen's law firm were so impressed that they'd offered her a part-time clerical job in the holidays. Must have been the expensive suit, I thought sourly. Tracie's tinies had cried when she left. (Secretly relieved, no doubt!) Simon had caught a thief and been praised by the store's owner. Two girls working at Dorothy Perkins had watched cute boys going into the store opposite and learnt how to shoplift from one of the salesgirls. Boffin-brain Andrew had spent a week in a garden centre lifting bags of compost and actually developed muscles.

Somebody asked me how I got on. I said OK and continued sorting my books. I waited for Lee. Two minutes before the bell for registration, Lee came in. He slung his bag onto his desk. His friends and most of the girls went into rent-a-crowd around him. I remained at my desk. I wasn't sure what to do. Lee started talking about the cybercafé. Every now and then he glanced across the room at me. I couldn't read his expression, but it certainly wasn't hostile. It was weird. There was some invisible chemistry between us. Strange feeling. Boys generally ignore me—I'm not thin enough or pretty enough. Not 'fanciable'. Unless they're taking the mick out of me or my accent. Like Lee and Grant used to do. Maybe Lee had really changed, I thought, as Mr Richards came in with the register. Now Grant had gone, maybe we were about to become friends. As we left the room, Lee fell into step with me.

'Hi,' I said. 'You OK?'

Lee glanced quickly over his shoulder. 'We have to talk,' he muttered under his breath.

'Sure.'

'How about break? Outside the PE block.' Then he walked quickly away, catching up with Simon. I went to my first lesson. I thought, Wow! I have a 'date' with Lee Scott. Eat your heart out Tracie and everyone else who fancies him. As soon as the bell went for break, I got myself to the head of the canteen queue. I bought a peach flavoured spring-water drink and threaded my way through the playground crowd to the PE block. Lee was waiting by the double doors, the usual crew of girls in attendance. Lee pushed open one of the double doors. 'I have to talk to Annie,' he told them. 'Catch you later.' The fan club made 'oooh' noises. Pathetic. I ignored them.

I followed Lee into the PE block and along the corridor. The PE block smells of sweaty trainers and Lynx aftershave. I tried not to take deep breaths. Finally Lee stopped outside the gym. He spun round to face me.

'So . . . ' I began.

'Annie,' Lee said urgently, 'about Friday.'

'Yeah,' I said, 'I've been thinking about what you said and—'

Lee interrupted me. 'You haven't told anyone, have you?'

'No!' I exclaimed. 'Of course not. Credit me with some intelligence!'

'Good,' Lee said. 'That's good. Look, Annie, it's like this: I want you to forget it.'

'I'm sorry?' I stared at him in astonishment.

'I shouldn't have told you. I was upset, angry, stressed. Please, just forget it—OK?'

'You mean you're saying it wasn't true?'

Lee paused. He looked at me. Then he looked away.

'So it was true then—you did see Grant on the Internet. He was involved in some porn racket!' I exclaimed.

'Yeah—it's true all right.' Lee grimaced.

'So why do I have to forget it?' I asked, puzzled.

Lee hesitated.

'You are going to find out who's behind it?' I asked. 'Well, are you?' I persisted.

'Yes, of course I am,' Lee said crossly. 'What do you take me for?'

'Good,' I said. 'Then, you'll need help, won't you? So I'll help you. Like you said, it'd be better with two of us. I have some ideas already. Shall I tell you?'

Lee sighed, exasperated. Half closed his eyes. Then realizing, I suppose, I wasn't to be shaken off so easily, he tried the old charm routine on me. 'Annie, Annie,' he said, soothingly, 'don't take this the wrong way. I mean, I know Grant and me, we gave you a bit of a hard time when you came here, but it was never personal.' He paused. Leaned in towards me. Smiled down into my eyes. 'You understand that, Annie? Don't you.'

'Uhhh.' I was suddenly mesmerized by his brown eyes. 'I suppose . . . '

Lee went on. 'You see, I really want to do this on my own. Can you understand that? Just me. After all, Grant was my friend. I owe him.' I had never experienced the Lee Scott treatment before. It was like being caught in the headlights of a ten-ton truck. I could see why it had the desired effect on most girls. Unfortunately, I wasn't most girls.

'Look, I think we should discuss this more,' I said, dragging my brain away before it filled up with fluff. 'You can't ask for my help one minute and then say you made a mistake the next. What's going on here?'

Abruptly, Lee switched off the charm. He glared at me. 'God, you can't leave it, can you? OK, listen. Carefully. First, this isn't some fun-girly thing.'

'But . . . ' I protested indignantly. Fun-girly? Who the hell did he think I was?

Lee ignored me. 'It's serious. For real. It could be dangerous.'

'Yes, I had worked that out for myself.'

'And there's another thing,' Lee said. 'Even if I wanted help, which I don't, it's like . . . well, I'd probably ask Simon. Maybe Helen or Tracie.'

'Oh?' I said coldly. 'Why them, not me?' But I knew the answer even before Lee kindly spelled it out for me.

'Well, let's face it, Viking, you're not the most popular person on the planet, are you?'

'I'm sorry?'

'I don't want to be unkind but, well, you don't come from this country—which is OK, right . . . but you do seem to rub people up the wrong way, don't you?'

'Meaning what, exactly? That I have three heads? That being seen with me will ruin your street-cred?' I asked.

'Look, it's not personal.'

'No?' I said between gritted teeth. 'Sounds personal to me.' All of a sudden, I felt depressed. I knew I wasn't top of everyone's party list, but I'd never had it thrown in my face quite so cruelly. I'd really thought Lee had changed but I'd got it wrong. Nothing had changed. It never would. Nobody liked me. I was an outsider and I always would be.

And then, as I was struggling not to show my feelings on my face, the door of the PE office opened behind me and one of the young PE student teachers appeared carrying a box of Unihoc sticks. Lee took one look at her (blonde, slim, cheekbones a mile wide) wiped the scorn off his face and slipped effortlessly back into charm-mode. 'Hey, allow me,' he said, almost pushing me aside. He seized the box of sticks, at the same time giving her the same heart-melting smile. 'Can't have you straining yourself, can we.' The student teacher looked at him. Then she smiled and went pink.

The Lee Scott sex-god act. Turn on the charm. Watch them melt. I'd seen it so often. And despised it. He was so bloody manipulative. Suddenly, I was furious. And hurt. And humiliated. I remembered the chemistry I'd felt between us at morning registration. If there was any chemistry between us now, it was the sort that evacuated buildings. I swore at Lee in Norwegian, which made the student teacher go even pinker. Then I spun on my heel and stomped off.

But as the day went on, I stopped being angry and started thinking. I'd been prepared to help Lee find the people who killed Grant. I'd almost forgiven him for the past. I'd even felt sorry for him. And in return for all this, I'd been given the flick. Told to forget about it. And told I was unpopular and unliked. Great. *Tusen takk!* Now, I came to a decision. I'd try to find out who killed Grant. On my own. Because there were principles involved here. Nobody was going to patronize me because I was a girl or humiliate me because I wasn't thin and blonde. Nobody was going to treat me differently because I was from another country. Not ever. I remembered the old Norse heroines—strong in battle, brave women-warriors, better than men. I'd show bloody Lee I-think-I'm-a-babe-magnet Scott, I thought. And I'd show the rest of my class too!

At lunch, I decided to go and talk to Hayleigh Penney, Grant's cousin. Hayleigh was in Year Seven. She lived in the same street as Grant and I knew the Penneys were always in and out of each other's houses. They stuck together. I reckoned if I played my cards right, she'd give me an overview of Grant's life. Then I could focus in on some details. We're always being told in English: overview first, details second.

I found Hayleigh sheltering in a doorway with a gang of

little girls. The junior playground is at the far end of the school and the wind hits it full on. Kniving winds, I thought, like in the poem. Hayleigh was easily recognizable: all the Penneys had the same reddish hair and foxy features. I beckoned her over. Then I felt in my pocket and produced a Mars bar. Year Seven kids will do most things for chocolate. Hayleigh's eyes lit up. She unwrapped the bar and took a big bite.

'Fanx,' she said slushily.

'So how's things,' I said. I walked off a little. As I expected, Hayleigh came trotting after me like a small dog. 'All right,' she said, chewing.

'Really sorry about your cousin,' I went on. 'I was in his class.'

'Was you?'

'Did you go to the funeral?'

'Nah, Mum said we'd only cry. We went to the party after.'

'Lots of family and friends?' I suggested.

'Only us and Grant's mum and the boys.'

'No close friends, then.'

'No. Why?'

'Just asking.' We walked for a bit. 'He always had nice stuff, your cousin, didn't he?' I went on casually. 'I remember that lovely leather jacket. And the bike too. Must've had a good job.'

Hayleigh stopped chewing and started noisily sucking chocolate off her fingers. Ugh, I thought. 'Didn't have a job,' she said.

'So what did he do evenings and weekends?'

'He used to hang out with Lee Scott. I fancy him,' she confided, giggling. 'He's got a sexy bum.'

You poor misguided fool! I thought. 'Where did they go?' I asked.

'Town. Round each other's houses.'

'Right. And when he wasn't with Lee?'

Hayleigh shrugged her thin shoulders. 'Stayed in. Played on his computer.' She peered suspiciously up at me. 'Why d'you want to know?'

'Just passing the time of day,' I said. By now we'd done a complete circuit of the school and were back at the doorway where I'd found her. 'Hey, shall I tell Lee you fancy him?'

Hayleigh was instantly distracted. She went bright pink, 'Don't you DARE!' she squealed delightedly. I smiled cryptically. 'Maybe he'll find out anyway. Who knows.' I winked. 'Thanks for the chat, Hayleigh,' I said. 'See you around.'

It was a start. Over lunch, (a *small* tuna sandwich, pineapple yogurt, and an orange) I planned my next move. I needed to talk to Grant's mum, maybe see his room, pick up some clues as to where he went, who he met. But that would have to be very delicately handled.

After lunch, I decided to tackle my other problem. I took my overweight body back to the PE department. I needed inspiring. When I got there, Miss Baxter, my PE teacher, was pinning things to the noticeboard. You can always recognize PE staff: they wear baggy tracksuits, trainers, and have high ponytails. And they don't walk, they bound along like they're on springs.

'Hello, Annie,' Miss Baxter shouted (PE staff always shout—years of working on windy playing fields), 'coming out to play netball?'

'Not today, miss,' I said. Actually, I was surprised she knew me. I always ducked out of games. Bad period pains. I had them every Wednesday afternoon. She still hadn't sussed.

'You really ought to join the team,' Miss Baxter boomed, as she bounced off. 'Get rid of some of that flab.'

Gee thanks, I thought. Jump up and down on my ego, why don't you. But she had a point. I had put on a bit of weight lately. Even my cellulite had cellulite. Something had to be done. But I wasn't going to subject my body to the ridicule and snide comments of my fellow students if I could help it. I scanned the noticeboard for ideas. Then I saw a flyer: *NEW!!! The White House Fitness Centre. Aerobics, step, weights etc. Professional and fully trained staff.* Underneath in smaller letters I read: *Students—why not take advantage of our 2 months' free trial membership!* There was a tear-off slip at the bottom. *Fint!* I thought, excellent. Problem solved. I unpinned the notice and pocketed it. I'd get the school office to stamp it later.

After registration, we had Citizenship. We finished our work experience diaries. In my case, started it. I decided to begin on the last page and work back. That way, it looked like I'd written loads. Whilst we were writing, Mr Richards strolled around reading bits over our shoulders. I hate it when teachers do that. My mind blanks out and I forget how to spell simple words.

'You've written a lot, Annie,' Mr Richards remarked when he reached me.

'Yes, sir,' I said. I always agree with teachers. It saves having to think.

'So you enjoyed your placement after all?'

'Yes, sir.'

'There you are, I told you it might be interesting, didn't I!'

'Yes, sir.'

He strolled off, humming happily. It's good to create harmony. Behind me, I heard a sarcastic snort. It appeared to come from where Lee and his mates sat. The gender from outer space. I chose to ignore it.

The pen is mightier than the sword

Words have power. Like the witches' spells in *Macbeth*—we'd started reading *Macbeth* in class. Like the poems written by

First World War poets. Just words on a page. Yet able to create powerful images which, if you believed, could conjure up strange worlds, evoke feelings of horror or pity, even change lives.

I was thinking about the power of words as I sat at my desk on Wednesday morning, forging a note excusing me from afternoon school. Brain and pen working in complete harmony. A few lines of writing, a signature—supposed to be my mother's. Only words on the page. Not, perhaps, life-changing stuff. Hardly in the same ball-park as Shakespeare, but my teachers believe it every time. Maybe I'll go into writing fiction when I'm older.

I disliked having to do it, but it was the only way I could think of. I needed to go round to Grant's house without anyone from school knowing. I had to find out who Grant knew, what he did after school, where he went. In my imagination, I was following the footsteps of Sherlock Holmes: eliminate the possible, then whatever remains, however impossible, must be the correct solution. Not that Sherlock Holmes had my problems, I thought, signing my mother's name with a flourish. His great arch-rival Moriarty was not competing against him to solve the same crime.

I handed my note to Mr Richards at morning registration. As expected, he gave it a cursory glance, then wrote me out a permission slip. I didn't feel guilty. If he hadn't wised up to my scam, that was his problem. And I was only missing PE—not so much healthy exercise as group mortification. I had an early lunch, made an anonymous call to Grant's house on the student pay-phone to check his mum was there. Then I set off.

I'd never met Mrs Penney. She didn't come to parents' evenings or school events. Grant used to brag that she only came in to school when he was in serious trouble. Which meant she was there fairly often. I hoped she wouldn't recognize me or know who I was.

When I lived in Norway, my grandfather told me stories about the spirits who inhabited places to protect them from harm. We used to give them imaginary names: Skog the forest spirit, Foss the waterfall spirit. I'd only been in the Penney house two minutes before deciding that if it had a spirit, its name had to be Trist—sad. I had never been anywhere with such an unhappy atmosphere. Even the furniture seemed to cower against the walls. I explained to Grant's mum how I'd lent Grant some science notes which I needed back.

'I'm ever so sorry to bother you,' I said apologetically. 'But we've got our mocks in a couple of weeks and I need them to revise from.'

Grant's mum had small pale blue eyes and colourless over-permed hair that needed washing. It was early afternoon and she wore a shabby grey tracksuit and maroon slippers. I'd read of people letting themselves go. Now I was seeing it first hand.

'Sorry,' she said tonelessly, 'what did you say your name was again?'

'Kelly,' I lied. There were five Kellys in my year.

'Well,' she sighed, 'I don't know.'

'Please, Mrs Penney,' I pleaded. 'I really really need them.'

'All right,' she said finally. 'You can come and have a look for them.'

I followed her upstairs. At the top of the stairs, she stopped outside a closed door.

'That's his room there,' she said.

'Right,' I said. 'Is it OK for me to go in?'

Mrs Penney shrugged.

'Thanks. I'll be ever so quick,' I said, my hand on the doorknob. 'I expect they'll be in his bag.'

Mrs Penney nodded, then turned and shuffled back downstairs. I opened the door and went in.

Grant's room was like entering a time warp. His uniform still hung off the back of a chair. His computer and some textbooks were on a small table in one corner. On one wall were a couple of posters of half-naked cyberbabes with enormous breasts and thighs. By the window, a rowing machine and some weights. Nothing had been touched. Except for the bunk beds: the pillows and duvets had gone and both beds had been stripped down to the striped mattresses. I guessed nobody slept there now. I also noticed Grant's trainers had been lined up neatly in front of the wardrobe. Odd.

For a brief moment, I stood absolutely still, listening to the total silence, sensing the sadness closing around me like a grey blanket. Picking up the hints I was an unwelcome intruder. Then I reminded myself that I had a job to do. And very little time to do it in. There was no place for sentiment. So I began to go systematically through Grant's things. I didn't know what I was looking for. I just hoped something would turn up that might give me a lead. I flicked through Grant's books but found nothing. I opened his bag and explored the contents. Used sweet papers, detention slips and some exercise books with doodles on. A zipped sidepocket yielded a couple of condoms. Skanked after the Citizenship lesson on contraception, no doubt! I also found a small business card with *Jimmy*'s written on it and a phone number. I left the condoms, but slipped the card into my pocket.

Then I opened the wardrobe door. Grant's leather jacket was hanging at one end. Nothing in the outer pockets. In the inside pocket, I found a wad of twenty pound notes. I put them back. I wasn't a thief.

I was just looking for other areas to search, when I heard footsteps coming slowly up the stairs. I glanced frantically around, checking I'd returned everything to its correct place. I swore softly. If only I'd had longer. The footsteps stopped outside Grant's door.

'Did you find your notes?' Mrs Penney called out.

'Yeah, just coming,' I replied. I ran a swift visual check: desk, bag, cupboard, I'd looked everywhere. I'd found nothing. Pulling a face, I left the room, closing the door behind me. Mrs Penney stood on the landing, her face expressionless, hands hanging limply.

'Got them, thanks,' I said, smiling and patting my bag.

I followed her down, cursing myself for not finding anything. I wondered if I'd missed something obvious. Too late now to go back again. Mrs Penney opened the front door.

'Well, thank you so much. I really didn't mean to trouble you,' I said, thinking how I could extend my visit.

'He was a good boy,' she muttered, her eyes looking past me.

'Um . . . sure.'

'The kids miss him so much.'

'Yeah, must do.'

'Jason won't sleep in the room any more.' She sniffed and dragged her sleeve across her eyes. 'And Kyle keeps asking when his big brother'll come back.'

It wasn't fair. There was so much I wanted to ask. But I couldn't. It wasn't the right time. So I got on my bike and rode away. Behind me, I imagined the silence surging softly back into Grant's room, smoothing the living ripples I'd made, until nothing remained to disturb the frozen stillness. When I got back, I rang the number on the business card. No reply. I kept ringing it off and on, over the next few days. No joy. Whoever and wherever Jimmy was, he wasn't taking calls.

We all mean different things to different people. I remember when Princess Di was killed. My mum woke me with the news. We spent all day in front of the TV. Watching the crowds queuing to sign books of condolence. People crying and hugging each other. Only a short while before, everybody hated her for abandoning her kids for her new boyfriend; suddenly she was a tragic goddess who'd done good all her life. And if you dared say a word against her, you were in real trouble. I know. I did. I tried to point out the hypocrisy of it. Nobody spoke to me for days. Death is like that. You forget the bad and only remember good things. It makes you feel better, I guess.

The rehabilitation of Grant Penney started that week we returned from work experience. Without warning, the old Grant had disappeared. People began recreating him—without the bad bits. The boys went on about how great he'd been at football, how he'd been a good laugh, hadn't he? The girls said things like OK he used to be a pain but he'd kind of grown up recently. I kept out of it. Too many memories. Too many scars. But it was hard, because of what I knew about Grant. I wanted to tell them what had paid for the clothes, the bike. What the Real Grant Penney was into in his spare time. Sometimes I had to really bite down on my lip, remind myself knowledge is power, power equals control.

Definition of control: Keeping my mouth shut.

On Friday, we gave our Work Experience talks in English. Mrs Taylor gave us twenty minutes to make notes, then we had to go to the front, speak and get graded for our GCSE orals. I hate being the centre of attention. People staring at me makes me feel fat, so I was not looking forward to it. I knew I could have made my talk interesting but I decided not to tell everyone about Billy Donne. He was my secret. I wanted to keep him to myself. So when it was my turn, I just related the boring bits, majoring on washing up and clearing plates. That way, I could get it over with quickly with no awkward questions. And I succeeded. Most of the class stared out of the window. A few people actually yawned. There were no questions at the end. Even Mrs Taylor looked relieved when I returned to my place.

'Er . . . thank you, Annie,' she said. 'That was . . . very . . . '

'Boring?' somebody remarked. Everyone laughed.

'Now, now,' Mrs Taylor said, sighing. 'I'm sure Annie's tried her best. Right now, Kelly,' she went on, brightening visibly, 'come and tell us about Dorothy Perkins.'

At break, I went straight to the school office and got the secretary to stamp the form for the White House Fitness Centre. I'd been trying to forget about it. Not any more: halfway through the oral, I'd felt the safety pin fastening my skirt give way forcing me to speak with my elbows clamped to my sides to stop my skirt from falling down. It was embarrassing. Not that anybody had noticed—too busy falling asleep. It really made me cross that I'd been on this stupid diet for four days, but it wasn't working. I'd just have to bite the bullet and do some real exercise. I decided to go and register at the fitness centre on Saturday.

Saturday was also the day I got my allowance. I needed some stationery for school so I cycled into town in the morning. The high street was heaving with people with trays of poppies. I'd forgotten it was Remembrance Sunday. There'd been Sixth Formers selling poppies all week but I'd been too preoccupied to notice. This year I had reason to remember. I thought of Noel Clark and of Billy Donne and put £5 into the tin. Then I went to W. H. Smith, checked out the magazines and bought some folders. I followed this up by going into Benetton where I spent some time unfolding jumpers. A lot of underbrained Year Twelve label junkies work there on Saturday. I like to keep them busy.

After creating as much mess as I could, I went to Margie's, the camping and workwear shop where I buy most of my clothes. I bought a grey vest, matching jogging bottoms and a brown headband. If I was going to exercise in a real fitness centre, I thought, I might as well look the part. I felt so good after buying my stuff, I decided to celebrate the new me (yet to emerge) by having a double banana sundae at the Blue Dog café. And to show how committed and focused I was feeling, I didn't order whipped cream on the side.

The White House Fitness Centre was down a quiet side street just north of the shopping parade. It was a large, three-storey Victorian house appropriately painted white. I parked my bike in the car park at the back and went to check it out. The place had a good buzzy atmosphere. Loud music was playing and you could hear exercise machines and people shouting instructions. I stood in reception, feeling the pounds melting away. All the staff wore white tracksuits with blue WHFC logos and ID badges with their names on. I was impressed. If the PE department at school were more like this, I thought, even I might be interested.

I signed up for the 7 o'clock Monday aerobics workout and was given a booklet and a personal fitness card. I felt great. At long last, I was taking charge of my body. No longer would food be my master. *Gratulerer!* Well done.

On the way home, I stopped at the local newsagent. As it was Remembrance Sunday the next day, I wanted to buy something to give to Billy. I looked around for a bit and finally decided on some After Eights. *'Say thank you with a box of chocolates'*, said the poster above the till. Good idea. I was very grateful to Mrs Penney for letting me search Grant's bedroom. I went and got another box. I needed a reason for going back to Grant's house. Now, I had it.

■ In Flanders fields the poppies blow

I arrived at Elmfield House at 2.30 on Sunday, not realizing anything special was happening. The first indication that something was up came when I encountered Mrs Morrison hovering in Reception, wearing a smart suit and looking a bit flustered.

'Oh, Annie,' she exclaimed, 'I'm so glad you're here. I tried to ring you yesterday afternoon.'

My heart lurched. Had something happened to Billy? Mrs Morrison noticed my worried expression. 'Billy's fine,' she reassured me. 'I just wanted to check you were visiting today.'

'Right,' I said, wondering why I hadn't heard the phone. I knew I was in. Revising with my personal stereo on seemed a possible reason.

'We're having a party for Remembrance Sunday,' Mrs Morrison went on. 'We do it every year. I really hoped you'd drop by. Billy will be so pleased to see you. Go through, Annie, everybody's in the lounge.'

Nice of her to be so concerned about me, I thought. Mistakenly as it turned out.

A party. Great. I pushed the door to the lounge open, thinking of the parties I'd been to which all had certain things in common: loud music, drink, and fighting. Somehow, I didn't think it was going to be like that today. I was right.

The lounge was packed. There were all the residents in their smartest cardies, wearing poppies and sitting around the edge of the room whilst a fat lady played gloopy songs on a portable organ. Some embarrassed relatives stood around, trying to get their mums, dads, grans etc. to join in. A few were singing, but not the same song. It was all terribly jolly and false at the same time. I felt sad. Why couldn't the old people be left alone? A couple of old ladies waved shakily at me and warbled 'Hello, Betty!' I waved back, thinking, thank God nobody from school could see me. They'd have wet themselves laughing.

Billy was sitting in a chair by the window. He'd been dressed up in a posh shirt and tie which hung grotesquely around his skinny old neck. 'Hi, Billy,' I said, crouching down next to him. 'Enjoying the party?' Billy looked upset. I didn't blame him. I wouldn't want to be at a Remembrance Day party if I were him. It was cruel. I was surprised nobody had realized this.

'Don't worry,' I whispered, 'I'll get you back to your room as soon as I can.'

'Annie!' Mr Reeve emerged from the kitchen, carrying a loaded tray. 'How nice to see you. Funny, I was just saying to Sue the other day, I wonder how young Annie's getting on!'

I gave him a weak smile. 'I thought you didn't work weekends?'

'Not normally, I don't. But today is special.' Mr Reeve put the tray down. I gave it a quick glance and sighed. Whatever I thought about Mr Reeve (and I did) he was a brilliant cook. There were plates of scones and tarts. And a luscious white-iced cake with little red poppies and the words: 'Lest we forget' piped on it. I reminded myself I was on a diet and swore silently.

'Give you a hand?' I asked dutifully, but Mr Reeve shook his head.

'You stay here,' he said. 'Anyway,' he went on, lowering his voice, 'I think our guests have just arrived.'

'Uhh?'

'Oh, we like to do things properly,' Mr Reeve said, nodding at me. 'I saw the car pull up, so they'll be here in a second.' He gave me his irritating old-dog-with-a-secret look and disappeared into the kitchen. Guests? So that was why Mrs Morrison looked smart and worried. And I'd thought it was because of me. As if. I decided I'd better move Billy quickly, before these guests arrived. I went back to him and was just levering him carefully out of his chair when the door to the lounge opened and Mrs Morrison swept in, followed closely by the mayor with gold chain, his wife, minders in dark suits, and a couple of photographers. I took one look and decided to gatecrash my way out.

Fat chance.

The mayor headed straight for Billy and started talking to him. Or rather, talking at him. He went on and on about how wonderful it was to see him again on this special day and how well he looked. He spoke slowly and loudly, as if talking to a small and very stupid child and he kept calling Billy 'old chap' in a patronizing way. I was livid. I stood behind Billy's chair fuming inwardly, praying he would find his tongue and tell the pompous git where to stick himself. Of course he didn't. He simply stared up at the mayor, looking confused. Just when I thought I was about to explode with rage, Mrs Morrison interrupted.

'And this is Annie,' she said smoothly, smiling at the mayor. 'Annie comes from one of the local comprehensives. She did a week's work experience with us and she was so interested in Billy that she decided to visit him regularly.'

'Isn't that wonderful,' the mayor's wife gushed. 'I mean, when you think of young people today . . . ' She caught my eye and shut up. I do withering scorn to industrial strength.

'Can we get a photo of the three of you together?' one of the photographers asked the mayor, unzipping his camera and beckoning me forwards.

'No,' I said firmly, but everyone ignored me. It must have been something to do with the power of the press because within a nanosecond, I was crouching beside Billy whilst the cameras flashed away. Billy blinked, I scowled, the mayor slapped a big grin on his face and two minutes later, the whole group were on their way out again into the darkening November afternoon. Duty done. Photocall over.

'Well, wasn't that nice,' Mr Reeve said, appearing at my elbow with a cup of tea for Billy. 'With a bit of luck, you'll be on the front page of the local paper. We'll have to look out for you on Tuesday.'

Great, I thought, bitterly. That's really made my day.

I hadn't meant to go back to Grant's house quite so soon, but the thought of my photo being in the local paper altered my plans. My cover was about to be blown. After Tuesday, I wouldn't be able to pretend to be Kelly. I decided I'd have to call round on Monday. However, I knew I couldn't get away with faking another sick note quite so soon after the last one. I'd have to implement Plan B. So during Monday's registration, I complained vaguely to Mr Richards of a headache. Then at break, I slipped into the girls' toilets, carefully powdered my face with talcum and put brown eyeshadow round my eyes to make them appear hollow. My drama teacher would have been proud of me—I looked really ill.

The geography teacher was certainly convinced. He wrote me a sick note without giving me a second glance. I turned down an offer from Tracie to take me to the medical room and staggered out of the classroom, clutching my forehead bravely. A couple of minutes later, I was cycling out of the school gate. I knew none of my teachers would check up on me. I have a reputation for being honest and trustworthy. It's a good thing to have. Especially when you decide not to be.

Mrs Penney wasn't surprised to see me. I guess Grant had so many 'free periods' that she was used to the idea we came and went at odd hours of the day. I didn't even have to suck up either. She accepted the chocolates, even giving me a watery smile and invited me in. Just what I wanted. I followed her shuffling footsteps down the shabby hall and into the untidy, breakfast-littered kitchen.

'I was just making a cuppa,' Mrs Penney said, reaching listlessly for the kettle. The sink was overflowing with dirty dishes and the kitchen smelt of cat pee. The whole place had a grey unwashed aura. I perched on a stool, trying not to show my disgust.

'So,' I said, surreptitiously examining my cup for stains, 'things OK?'

Mrs Penney sighed. 'You kids—you're really kind,' she said. 'I mean, Lee's been round nearly every day.' She paused. 'Do you know Lee?' she asked. 'He goes to your school. He was Grant's best friend—been together since primary school.'

'No,' I lied, shaking my head. 'He's not in any of my sets.'

'Well, he's ever such a nice boy. Really good to me. I think he feels bad because he wasn't there for Grant at the end.' She paused and fished a hanky out of her grubby sleeve. 'None of us was . . . ' her voice tailed off helplessly.

'So Grant didn't leave a note?' I asked.

'Nothing,' Mrs Penney sniffed. 'No note, no letter, not a thing. The police went through everything with a fine-tooth comb, believe me. That's how we knew it was an accident.'

'He used to talk about a place called Jimmy's,' I remarked casually.

'Oh yes, he went to Jimmy's a lot,' Mrs Penney said. My heart leapt.

'He said it was really good. I thought I might go.' I tried to keep my voice steady. 'Near here, is it?'

'Over Springfield Estate, I think,' Mrs Penney said. She levered herself out of her seat. 'I think Grant had a card in his bag. I'll go and fetch it.'

'Er, no, really it's OK,' I said quickly. 'I'll find it, honest. I'm good at finding places.' I gulped down my tea and stood up. 'Thanks again for letting me get my notes,' I said. 'I really appreciate it.'

'Well . . . if you're sure,' Mrs Penney said doubtfully.

'No worries,' I said firmly.

She showed me to the door. 'Come again, Kelly,' she said. 'Any friend of Grant's is always welcome.'

I got my bike and wheeled it to the gate. Mrs Penney stood in the doorway watching me. I felt sad for her. What did she know? What would she do when she did? Life's a bitch, I reflected. I turned the corner and cycled back to school. I timed my arrival to coincide with the end of lunchbreak. There are always kids coming back from home. It was easy to slip in amongst them. Mr Richards was pleased to see me.

'Feeling better, Annie?' he asked.

'Yes, sir,' I said meekly, making my way to my desk. As I

sat down, I caught Lee's eye. For a moment, I held his gaze steadily. He looked away. *Fint!*

During afternoon class, I thought about what I'd found out so far. A brief mental overview. I knew how Grant had died. I knew where and when. I knew why. But that was all. Jigsaw pieces. Nothing fitted together. I was several big bits missing. Maybe I'd find them at Jimmy's.

After school, I went to the Drama Studio. I had a practical coming up. I needed to sort out some stuff. I messed around with the box of stage make-up for a bit, trying out different things on myself and making a few helpful notes. Then I packed up. I cut through B block, now deserted and quiet. There was a light on in my form room. The door was slightly open. I could see someone sitting at the teacher's desk. I called out 'Night, sir,' as I passed. Nobody answered. Halfway down the stairs, I paused, thought for a bit and went quietly back again.

Lee Scott jumped up as I pushed open the door. But not before I'd seen his hand in Mr Richards's drawer. He glared at me.

'What the hell are you doing here?' he snapped.

'So—I might ask you the same question.'

'None of your business. Anyway, it's my form room.'

'Yeah, it's my form room too.'

Lee made like he was about to leave. I blocked his way.

'Why were you going through Mr Richards's desk?' I asked.

Lee pulled a face. 'I wasn't.'

'Oh, give me a break! I saw you.'

Lee sighed. 'Look, it's not what you think.'

'Sure it isn't.'

'I mean it.'

'Right. And Mr Richards will be OK about it tomorrow, yeah?'

'He's not going to know.'

'Oh, I think he'll find out, somehow,' I said. I smiled. I remembered Lady Macbeth's advice about flowers and serpents.

Lee swore again.

'Not a chance,' I said, still smiling. I was enjoying this. Lee owed me big time. 'So what's going on?'

Lee sighed. 'What do you think?' he said.

I shrugged. 'You tell me.'

'I'm looking for evidence, of course.'

'Sorry?'

'Grant. I was looking for evidence. Photos, lists, I don't know. Something, anything.'

'*Mr Richards!*' I exclaimed. 'Are you crazy?'

'It could be him,' Lee said, determinedly. 'He had the opportunities, didn't he? Saw Grant every day. And after school for detention.'

'But he's a teacher!' I gasped.

'So?' Lee said. 'Doesn't mean he's any different to anyone else.'

'He's going out with Miss Dalton.'

'All the more reason. Needs the money.'

I was shocked. I liked Mr Richards, even though he dressed like a refugee from Oxfam. 'I think you've lost the plot,' I said firmly.

'Right,' Lee sneered, 'and you're an expert.'

'No, but I know teachers don't do that sort of thing.'

'Yeah? So what about the guy from that posh school who took porno pictures of boys?'

I remembered that. It'd been in the papers recently.

'See,' Lee said, watching my face. 'Not so sure now, are you?'

'But Mr Richards . . . ' my voice tailed off. I frowned. No, it couldn't be. Mr Richards was too nice. Too normal. He didn't fit into my jigsaw.

'No, I don't believe it,' I said, shaking my head. 'He'd be

crazy to try anything with someone in his own form. I mean, we'd find out.'

'Yeah?' Lee said. 'Then how do you explain this?' He bent down and handed me a magazine. I looked at the cover and grinned.

'That's your evidence, is it?' I said. 'Mr Richards has a girly mag in his desk, so he must be running a porn racket. Right. Brilliant assumption. Only one thing wrong with it . . . '

'What?'

'I happen to know he confiscated it from one of the Year Eights on Friday. He was telling us in History. We all saw that mag. He showed us. Ask Helen. She was there.'

Lee's face fell. 'Shit!' he muttered.

'So what were you going to do with it?' I went on. 'Take it to the police? Nice one.'

Lee opened a drawer and replaced the mag. 'Anybody can make a mistake,' he said crossly.

'A mistake like that could've cost him his job,' I told him.

Lee grimaced. 'OK. You don't have to go on.'

'You should be more careful,' I remarked, turning to go. 'Breaking into teachers' desks. Accusing innocent people.' I shook my head slowly and sadly. 'Oh dear, oh dear. Maybe you should give up.'

'No way,' Lee snapped. 'I'll find out who did it. It's only a matter of time.'

I smiled to myself. He was right. It was only a matter of time. But I was the one who was going to find out who killed Grant Penney. Not Lee Scott.

■ Some days you're the statue, some days the pigeon

Tuesday morning, I woke up feeling great. Now I knew

why people became exercise junkies. I'd really enjoyed my first session at the fitness centre. Everyone had been friendly and attentive and Stacey, my class leader, had given me my own personal mantra to say whenever I felt I needed encouragement. It was: *my body is a lean, mean, fighting machine*. I repeated it as I showered and dressed. I said it some more as I ate my bowl of oatmeal, brown sugar, and chopped bananas.

Another reason I felt good was because of Lee. Maybe I hadn't discovered who was behind Grant's death, but at least I knew Lee hadn't either. And if he was fingering our tutor, then he was way off the mark. Today I was going to enjoy seeing him squirm. He'd be really worried about me telling Mr Richards. Of course I wouldn't. I have principles. I don't dob. But I'd let him suffer a bit. No, a lot. Serve him right, the creep. I wondered whether Lee had discovered Jimmy's yet. Given he and Grant were such good mates, it'd only be a matter of time. But the chances of him getting anywhere were doubtful. He wouldn't know what questions to ask. Lee Scott was a loser. I said it a few times as I packed my bag. I'd made up another mantra—I was on a roll. Even my safety-pin seemed looser as I cycled to school. I felt like punching the air and shouting.

In the afternoon, Mrs Taylor kept me back after English class. 'I wonder if you might be interested in this, Annie,' she said giving me a book. 'I went to a car boot sale at the weekend and bought it. There's a poem in it by that First World War poet Noel Clark—are you still interested in him?'

'Yeah, I am.' I nodded.

'I thought you might like to read it.'

'Thanks,' I replied, 'thanks a lot.'

'It's on page 18,' she said.

I flipped open the book and read:

The Poster

'Join today!' the poster sang,
A tapestry of life so bright.
The young man's eyes were mesmerized
As moths allured by fire at night.
The noble soldier on the wall
Would lead him out of boredom's trench,
To leave the stifled English lawns
For new, exciting pastures French.

Now not a single day is dull;
In chilling mud he bends his knees,
His rat-hole reeks of chivalry:
A knightly cote of lice and fleas.
Excitement stabs in trembling fits
And every moment holds surprise.
How vividly he now recalls
Those garish, staring poster eyes.

'It's different to the other poems,' I said, thoughtfully.

'I thought that too,' Mrs Taylor agreed. 'It reminded me of a poem by Siegfried Sassoon—you remember the one beginning: "I knew a simple soldier boy".'

I nodded. I repeated a couple of lines. Mrs Taylor's eyes brightened.

'Well done,' she exclaimed. 'I did teach you something.'

'It's like he feels really bitter and betrayed,' I said.

'"The hell where youth and laughter goes",' Mrs Taylor quoted. 'Yes, that's exactly the feeling.' She looked at me and smiled. 'You can borrow the book if you'd like to, Annie.'

'Yeah, I would like to. Thanks,' I said again. I slipped it into my rucksack and went to get my bike. When I got home, I decided to copy out the poem and pin it to my wall with the other ones. I'd just finished when I heard the letterbox open and something land on the hall mat. The local paper. I'd almost forgotten about it. I went downstairs. I expected the photo of the Remembrance Day party would probably be stuck out of sight on an inside page where nobody'd see it.

In my dreams!

I picked up the paper, took one look and my heart sank. It was all over the front page. Me, the mayor, and Billy. Under a big banner headline: THREE GENERATIONS CELEBRATE PEACE TOGETHER. The mayor was grinning away, showing all his teeth. He reminded me of the wolf about to eat Little Red Riding Hood. Billy looked asleep—the camera had caught him mid-blink. As for me—I'm not photogenic at the best of times. My face is too fat. My cheeks stick out. My eyes disappear. And I always scowl. The photo made me look really rough—I could have won a Freak of the Millennium award, no contest. To make it worse, they'd spelled my name correctly, so I couldn't pretend it was somebody else. Hot damn! From pigeon to statue in less than ten hours. It was a tragedy. There was only one thing to do. Ignoring my mantra and obeying my deepest instincts, I headed for the fridge.

Wednesday was not a good day. Some people enjoy the limelight. I'm not one of them. Some people like being mentioned in Upper School assembly. I don't. Some people get a kick out of seeing press stories about themselves displayed on the Head's Newsboard in the foyer. I can live without the glory. For a while, I was slightly amused by the way everyone treated me as if I was Mother Theresa. Then the novelty wore off and I got angry because they kept referring to Billy as if he was a vegetable, not a human being. 'Aw, poor old thing,' Tracie kept saying. 'Isn't he cute,' Helen added. I thought of the quiet suffering I'd often seen in Billy's eyes and felt my fingers twitch.

I never went home for lunch, but that day, I did. I had to get away from the cloying sentimentality so at odds with the truth. And I felt my private space had been violated. Billy was mine. Part of my personal life. Now everybody knew him. Or thought they did.

I was angry. With the papers. With my fellow students. With myself for agreeing to the photocall. I got home, made myself a peanut butter and mashed banana sandwich and took it and a glass of milk up to my room. I sat on my bed eating my lunch and imagining what I'd do to everyone if I had the chance. Especially the journos. Poor Billy, I thought. Robbed of his dignity. Not that he'd ever realize. There were advantages to living in your own head. Me, I still had the afternoon to get through.

However, fate/God offered an unexpected lifeline: it began to snow. By period four, when the first flakes appeared, drifting out of a lead-coloured sky, people were complaining of the cold. The radiators were barely warm. Suddenly, I was no longer interesting. I had been replaced by something far more important: the weather. It always amuses me the way people take weather so seriously here, especially anything unusual, like snow. This country can't handle snow. In Norway, it's part of life. Sometimes it gets so cold, we throw warm water in the air to watch it becoming a cloud of ice crystals before it hits the ground. Last year, the temperature in Karasjok fell to minus 51.2C. Planes were frozen to the runway. Mobile phone networks collapsed. That's real snow. Here it's more like pavement dandruff.

I mentioned this to a few moaners and got the usual glares accompanied by muttered comments. But I didn't mind. I was relieved. Saint Annie had fallen from her pedestal!

On Thursday, I woke up to a white world. More snow had fallen overnight. Like a good student, I dutifully tuned in to the local radio station, crossing my fingers. My luck was in: school was closed. No heating. I saw my mother off to work. Then I settled in front of the TV in my dressing gown, with a hot chocolate and a plate of raisin toast. *Tusen takk!* Just what I needed. By Friday, everyone would have forgotten the article. It was only a week before study leave for our Mocks. Soon it would be the holidays. All I had to do was lie low and keep quiet.

I made a mental list of everything I intended to accomplish today: from revise quadratic equations, through start *Macbeth* essay, finishing up with check out Jimmy's. The snow was still falling so I decided to leave that last one until the afternoon. It would be a long bike ride across town in the snow.

■ I'm a big kid about Christmas

Give me lots of snow—the powdery sort—decorated shops, little iced spice cakes and I'm in heaven. Every year I'm the same. Even in England. Although, if I have a criticism of Christmas over here, it has to be not enough reindeer. Norway is full of reindeer. I really miss them at Christmas. Reindeer are good, especially with fried potatoes. It took me a long time before I could listen to 'Rudolph the red-nosed reindeer' without feeling hungry.

Jimmy's was not what I'd expected. For a start it was on an industrial estate—very difficult to find. I had to constantly ask directions. The outside looked like an old warehouse. There were no windows and the only indication I'd finally found it was when I spotted a card with 'Jimmy's' stuck on a wall with Sellotape. I pushed open the door and went in. The place smelled of paint and the floor looked to have been recently sanded. There was no indication what went on. Nobody to ask, no reception desk, just an empty white-painted corridor with a phone on the wall. Why did Grant come here? I stood wondering what to do next.

At last, I heard footsteps and the swing doors that led off the corridor swung open. A huge black man in tracksuit and vest appeared. He stood propped against the open doorway, chatting on his mobile. I could hear hammering coming from behind him. And another sound that I couldn't quite identify. At first, the black guy didn't notice me, too engrossed in his call. When he finally saw me, he stopped, muttered something and stuck the phone in his side pocket.

'Hi? Can I help you?' As he walked over to me I suddenly realized that I was a lot shorter than I felt!

'Er . . . yes, right,' I stuttered. This guy had muscles like mountain ranges.

'You looking for someone?'

'Sort of. I mean, like maybe.' My sharp, carefully rehearsed speech seemed to have vanished, to be replaced by verbal fluff.

'Mmmm-hmmm.' The guy leaned against the wall, casually folded his arms and looked me up and down. His biceps rippled under his black skin. I stared at the floor, feeling myself going red.

'Now, what's a cute girly like you doing round here?' he drawled. I have a nice line in biting sarcasm specially reserved for people who patronize me. Somehow, I didn't think using it on this guy was a wise move.

I was just contemplating my next move when the door swung open again to reveal another man, dressed in a smart suit. He was white, late twenties, early thirties. I'm not good at ages. He was good-looking though, blue eyes, square jaw. His dark hair was tied back in a ponytail. 'Curtis? You done yet?' he asked.

'Just coming, Jimmy.'

The man held the door, waiting. The hammering continued intermingled with the other noise—a sort of rhythmical thumping accompanied by groans. Suddenly, I realized what it was: the sound of someone getting a beating. Omigod, I thought, what the hell is this place?

'I thought I said no girlfriends whilst you're working,' Jimmy said, staring at me.

'Hey, boss, she's not my girlfriend, she just came in for something,' Curtis replied.

'OK, I'll take over. You get back to the client,' Jimmy ordered. Curtis nodded at me, grinned and disappeared through the swing doors. Client? I thought. Was that something to do with the beating up?

'Er . . . I'll be getting along then,' I muttered, edging towards the exit. All at once, I'd lost interest in Jimmy's. Whatever Grant had done here, I didn't want to know.

'Hang on,' the man called Jimmy said. He beckoned me over, smiling. 'Don't run away.' He had a nice smile. 'You mustn't let Curtis put you off. He likes teasing people. Good in the ring, but lacking in social graces. So, what can I do for you?' I noticed how very blue his eyes were. If he'd been a bit younger and I hadn't heard what was going on in the background, maybe I would have fancied him. As it was, I looked at the floor and mumbled: 'Umm . . . someone I know recommended this place. I was thinking of, like, joining.'

'Really?' Jimmy's eyes widened in astonishment.

'Er . . . yeah. Is that a problem?'

'Well, not a problem, more . . . unusual. We haven't had any women wanting to fight before.'

'Fight?' I exclaimed, my mouth dropping open in surprise.

'Yes. This is a boxing club. Of course, I'm sure we could accommodate you—what weight did you think of coming in at?'

Boxing! So that was what Grant did. Right. Now I understood the hitting noise I'd heard. And the reference to Curtis being good in the ring. For a while back there I thought I'd stumbled across a branch of the Mafia.

'Ah—*boxing* . . . ' I said, nodding.

'Yes—didn't your friend tell you?'

'Ugh—well, he was a bit vague,' I bluffed. 'I got the

impression you taught martial arts—t'ai chi, that sort of thing. Must have misheard. Yeah—my mistake. Should have listened. Well, there you go.' I rambled on a bit whilst I considered my next move.

'This friend . . . ' Jimmy interrupted me, 'does he come here regularly?'

'Er . . . not sure,' I said. 'Grant Penney—do you know him?'

Jimmy's smile widened. 'Grant!' he exclaimed. 'You know Grant?'

'He goes to the same school,' I admitted. 'Went,' I corrected myself. 'He wasn't a friend or anything.'

Jimmy's expression altered. 'Yes, I heard about what happened,' he said dropping his voice. 'Bad business.'

'Yeah.'

'Suicide, wasn't it?'

I nodded.

'Stressed out at school the papers said. They work you kids too bloody hard.'

I wasn't going to argue with that.

'Mind, I hadn't seen Grant for months,' Jimmy went on.

'No?'

'I've been abroad on business. America. Only got back a couple of days ago.'

'Right,' I nodded.

'Tell you what . . . sorry, I don't think I know your name?'

'Annie.'

'Annie—got it. I was really gutted when I heard the news about Grant.'

'Yeah.' It felt weird talking about somebody who was dead.

'One of the punters told me. Really cut me up. I mean, you kids, you got your whole lives ahead of you.'

'Right.'

We stood for a minute in respectful silence. Like at a funeral. Then Jimmy said: 'So, Annie, t'ai chi—do you think there'd be a take-up for it?'

My heart leapt. This was the chance I wanted. Now I'd have a reason to come back. Check the place out for myself. 'I'm sure.' I nodded.

'OK, leave it with me. I'll see what I can do.'

'Shall I ring you?' I asked.

'If you like. Give it a week or so, eh. I'll have to get round my contacts.'

'That'd be great,' I said, turning to go. 'Thanks.'

'No worries. You stay in touch, now.'

'Sure.'

On the way home, I stopped off at Marks and Spencer and rewarded myself with a chicken tikka in pitta bread and a Pineapple and Grapefruit Bliss. I deserved it. I was really pleased with myself: I'd handled things well. I was making progress.

On Friday, the heating was fixed. School reopened. The brief, unseasonal snowfall turned into grey slush. The teachers moaned at us for messing up their floors. As if we did it deliberately. A week to go before study leave and teachers were getting jittery. By mid-week we were all sick of it and moaning too.

'What do they think we're going to do?' Helen asked. 'Leave the country?'

'I wish,' one of the girls sighed.

'Don't they trust us to work?' Helen went on indignantly, drumming her fingers on the desk.

No, they didn't. I'd got so many 'revision guides' it would take me longer to read through them than do the actual work.

'It's the way they keep going on about last year's Year Eleven too,' Helen sniffed. 'So, they worked; so, they did OK. Who cares? They should be concerned about us.'

It was true. We were constantly being told we weren't as 'committed' as the year above us. It was disheartening.

'You're right. At least nobody in our year's got pregnant or been expelled for drugs,' Simon said. We knew who he was referring to. Last year's Year Eleven were not all angels. Trouble was, teachers had short-term memories.

'Yeah, what've we done to stress them out?' Tracie asked. Nobody answered. Nobody mentioned Grant. I thought: maybe teachers weren't the only ones who conveniently forgot.

'If they're so worried about us, why are they letting us go on study leave?' Helen went on. She was well into her stride now. 'They should keep us in school. Make us work normal lessons.'

'I think they like the free time,' I put in. 'Miss Mitchell says she can't wait to see the back of us.'

This was a slightly generous interpretation. What she'd actually said was: 'Annie, I can't wait to see the back of you.'

'That's what I mean,' Helen said, twisting a strand of hair round and round her fingers. 'One minute they're on our case, the next they couldn't give a toss. I hate all the bloody teachers in this school.'

It is said that one in five teenagers suffers from some sort of stress. I'd read that in the newspapers. I didn't have to look far to identify the statistic in our midst. Mind you, I was lucky. I didn't have Helen's pressures. She was predicted to get A or A* in all her subjects. I might scrape an A in English and Biology. Beyond that, it was anybody's guess. Helen's mother was always coming in to see Mr Richards about her progress. I had to leave my mother post-it notes to remind her about parents' evenings. A couple of times, she forgot. Pressure of work. In adults, the stress rate is higher.

'Well, it will soon be Christmas,' I said, trying to look on the bright side. On my way to school I'd seen men putting up the Christmas lights in town.

'Thanks, Annie! That's really good to know!' Helen snapped savagely. She got up from her seat and stalked out, slamming the door behind her.

Tracie gave me a reproachful look. 'You know she doesn't like talking about Christmas. It reminds her of when her mum and dad split up,' she hissed. Everyone looked at me accusingly.

'So?' I said, glaring round. No one answered. I buried my nose in a book. Maybe I didn't like talking about Christmas either. It brings back too many memories. My grandfather's wrinkly old face softened by candlelight, the taste of oven-warm gingerbread and my father lifting me up to the window to count stars in the velvet black sky. But nobody was interested in my feelings, of course.

Geography was a carbon copy of every other lesson we'd had that week. Nagging and moaning, followed by Helpful Hints, which, broken down, consisted of more nagging and moaning. I was beginning to see Helen's point of view. Even I was getting pissed off. And I'm not a stress freak. However, I reminded myself that it was only two more days. Then I'd be free to organize my life. Lose weight, maybe have my hair cut differently. And I could phone Jimmy's. Work on my investigation a bit more. Unlike Lee. He'd have nothing to work on. No teachers' desks to raid after Friday!

■ There is no pleasure so great as watching a man fall off a roof

The Chinese philosopher Confucius said that. I don't remember when he said it, but ever since I'd caught Lee snooping through Mr Richards's desk, I knew what he meant. It was most enjoyable. That feeling of *schadenfreude*. I knew I shouldn't be enjoying it so much but I was.

Lee and I hadn't met face to face for days—he'd definitely

been avoiding me. However, when I went to get my bike, I ran across him getting his. 'Hello, Lee,' I said airily. 'Checked out any more *desks* recently?' I grinned at him, noticing how he sucked in his breath and glanced quickly round to check nobody was about.

Lee gave me a venomous look. 'No,' he snarled.

'Just as well.' I undid my padlock and eased my bike off the stand. 'Only I still think I should have told somebody. For security reasons, you understand.' I paused. 'Nothing personal,' I said with heavy emphasis.

Lee pulled a face. Way to go, Annie, I thought. I'd waited a long time for this. Now I was going to savour every single moment of his discomfort. Revenge is a dish best tasted cold.

'In my country, we respect other people's property,' I continued. This was not strictly true, I'd had stuff nicked at my primary school in Oslo. Kids are kids the world over. But it sounded good and Lee wasn't to know. 'And we respect each other as well,' I added, for good measure.

'Yeah, OK. I get the message. Can we drop it,' Lee said. People were arriving to collect their bikes.

'Well, I don't know,' I said, raising my voice for maximum coverage. 'Like you said, anybody can make a mistake. Maybe I made one. Maybe I should have gone straight to the Head of Year and told her what you did. But how would I know, I'm just a stupid "girly".'

The other students getting their bikes looked quickly across at us and then went into Oh-look-I've-just-discovered-some-dust-on-the-front-wheel mode.

'OK,' Lee hissed. 'I get the message. What do you want—blood?'

'An apology might be nice,' I said, my voice dripping icicles. 'For starters, that is.'

Lee looked at me. 'This isn't just about Mr Richards, is it?' he said.

'Wow! Aren't you the bright one,' I replied. There were a

few sniggers from behind me. Everybody enjoys a good slagging match. I noticed that the crowd was growing by the second as word zipped round the school. Good. For once in my life, I wanted an audience.

'So what's it about then?' Lee said.

'Don't you know?'

'I just told you, didn't I.'

'If you don't know, I'm not going to tell you.'

Lee groaned. 'Oh come on, Viking. Don't play games. You're obviously mad at me about something.'

'My name,' I told him coldly, 'is Annie. Annie. Can you try to remember that? Or are you stupid as well as a thief.' There was the sound of indrawing breath from the onlookers.

'It's OK—she doesn't know what she's talking about,' Lee told them.

Oh really?

I got on my bike. 'Ask him,' I addressed the crowd. I pointed at Lee. 'Go on. Ask him about Mr Richards's desk. Ask him what he was doing the other afternoon. And why. See what he says.' Then I pushed my bike roughly through. Behind me, I could hear Lee launching into his explanation.

'It's OK. It's nothing,' he was saying. 'She got hold of the wrong end of the stick, that's all . . . ' I smiled to myself. Let him sort it out, I thought. Of course he would. I knew that. And they'd believe him. He was too plausible and too popular. I'd never really 'win' against Lee or any of the others, but the occasional small victory felt very very good.

That evening, I made an elaborate revision chart. I blocked in the week and filled it with subjects. I used my special colours for the days, the ones I see in my mind: Monday is pale grey, Tuesday—orange, Wednesday—apple green, Thursday—purple, and Friday, dark brown. I've associated colours with days of the week since I was very young. Apparently, it is a recognized psychological phenomenon. It has a name—though I can't remember it. My classmates have a name for it too: bloody stupid! It made me feel optimistic though, like I was really going to work hard and achieve good grades.

Later, I decided to revise some English. I got out my anthology and reread the First World War poems. Even after dissecting them in class, I still felt moved to tears as I read. Naturally, I started thinking about Noel Clark and then about Billy Donne. One had purged his suffering through his verses, the other had buried it deep inside. In my mind, the two had now become inextricably linked: a fusion of words and silence. A dead poet and a living soldier. I don't know when the idea that maybe there was something more first hit me. Maybe subconsciously, I had been thinking it ever since the day I met Billy. Now, it got me thinking about them again.

Of course I realized it was statistically impossible: thousands of men died on those godforsaken fields. The chance of two lives intersecting, however briefly, was remote. Yet odder things happened: angels had appeared at the battle of Mons. It was possible in some past existence, barely dignified by the word 'life', the two might have met. And now, in the strange world of cause and effect, I had entered the equation, pulling past and present together. The butterfly and the tidal wave. The unconnected connect.

I thought about it for a long time. Like a mathematical problem, I could see a possible outcome but not the way to reach it. Then I had an idea: on Sunday, I would show Noel Clark's poems to Billy. I would link him to the past. Perhaps this would be the key to unlocking the door of his silence.

I woke up on Thursday with a headache and stomach cramps. It's great being a woman! My shoulder felt stiff too. I must have lain on it awkwardly. I lurched into the shower, feeling 100 years old. I ate some muesli and grated apple and struggled to school. The sun was trying to break through the low cloud cover as I turned in at the gate. I reminded myself that it was only two days to study leave. I parked my bike and lugged my heavy bag painfully across to B block. I was not in a good mood. A small group from my class was hanging out in the foyer. Lee was amongst them. I stalked past, head held high.

'Morning, *Annie*,' Lee greeted me with exaggerated emphasis. I gave him a 'drop dead' look.

'Oooh, *Annie*'s still cross with me,' Lee grinned, unabashed. He clutched Simon in pretend fear.

'Don't bother with her,' simpered Tracie—the Lee Scott groupie.

'So who asked for your opinion?' I snarled viciously. I'm mean when I'm menstrual.

'Sorree.' Tracie's eyes widened. 'Pardon me for living.'

I turned away and began to climb the stairs to my form room.

'Hey, Annie, I remembered your name,' Lee called tauntingly after me. 'Annie . . . Annie.'

I ignored him. My head was throbbing and the strap on my bag was cutting into my shoulder. I conjured up a whole bunch of awful things I'd like to happen to Lee. Top of the list? Reincarnation as a woman with bad period pains. I felt no better by break. Some months I get like this. So I went to the sick bay. I spent the rest of the morning curled up in a foetal position with a hot water bottle for comfort. It's good to get out of the food chain every now and then.

After lunch, which I didn't eat, so I knew I was sick, the school nurse let me go home. I went to my form room to get my books. Helen was there, stressing to Mr Richards. The rest of my class had left for their first lesson. I loaded my bag with the books I needed for the evening.

'I'm going home,' I told Mr Richards on my way out. 'Stomach cramps.' Mr Richards never questions stomach cramps. I think he's embarrassed.

'Oh dear. Hope you feel better soon, Annie,' he replied, sympathetically. I grunted.

'Hey, Annie, wait up,' Helen called out to me. I stopped in the corridor and waited for her to come out. I wondered what she wanted me for. I didn't think she was going to ask me how I was. Not her style. I must have transgressed another unwritten law. Finally, Helen emerged. She looked around, saw me and strode over, looking cross. I felt a slight sinking in the pit of my stomach. It didn't go with the period cramps. 'OK, Annie—what have you got against Tracie?' Helen asked aggressively thrusting her face close to mine. 'She was really upset this morning.'

My mouth fell open. 'Excuse me?'

'Why did you have to slag her off? And in front of Lee. She was devastated.' It was amazing the way Helen and Tracie stuck up for each other. Even when they were totally out of order.

'Whoa—hold it right there,' I replied. I could feel my shoulders and jaw going tight. 'As I recollect it, I was talking to Lee. Private conversation. She pushed in. Sorry. Not my problem.' Faced with conflict, I start thinking in Norwegian. My English goes monosyllabic. It makes me sound cold and standoffish which is not always the impression I want to give, though I didn't mind that right now.

'You're always picking on her, aren't you?' Helen went on, her eyes two mean slits. 'Like, she rang you on work experience and you were rude to her. She told me about it.'

'Huh?' I was so taken aback by this that my words were sucked into an indignant black hole in my brain leaving me speechless.

'We've all tried to be nice to you,' Helen continued. 'But you've got a real attitude problem. You slag us all off, you go on about how wonderful Norway is and how crap it is here. What's your problem?'

'I think it's you who have the problem,' I replied stiffly.

‘Listen,’ Helen sneered, ‘if you don’t like it here—go back to your own country. You’ll be doing us all a big favour.’ She glared at me, spun on her heel and marched up the corridor, her back bristling with anger and self-righteousness.

I stared after her thinking: bitch! I waited till she was out of sight. Then I doubled back to my form room and got the rest of my books. The place was pissing me off. The people were pissing me off. I’d had enough. Time for a little distance learning. I loaded my bike and set off home. Maybe I’d come back for my exams. Maybe I wouldn’t.

They say home is where the heart is, although in my case, the location of the fridge is also important. As soon as I got home, I dumped all my stuff in the hallway and went straight to the kitchen. Anger makes me hungry. And I’d had no lunch. So I fixed myself a ham and Swiss cheese sandwich on rye bread with salad, mayonnaise, and pickle. I filled a bowl with organic vanilla icecream topped with fresh lemon sauce. I added a big glass of spring water and a banana. When the going gets tough, the tough get eating.

I took my food up to my room. Put on some music. Chilled out. After a while, I felt much better. Words can only hurt if you let them. I wasn’t going to let them. Especially words from creeps like Helen or Lee, who were so up themselves they’d probably got love-bites on their mirrors.

Sunday was one of those warm golden days that make you forget winter is just around the corner. Billy was sitting in the garden when I arrived at Elmfield. A few other residents were also toasting their dry old bones in the hazy afternoon sunshine. I perched on the arm of the bench and chatted to them about the unseasonal weather. The oldies discussed weather endlessly. I thought about explaining my theories on computers and global warming, but decided not. It would only unsettle them. After a while, one of the weekend staff came out with a tray of tea—the other hot topic of conversation.

Eventually, the sun dipped and it started to get cold. We all went inside. I accompanied Billy as he shuffled slowly to his room. 'Look, I brought something to show you,' I told him when I'd got him comfortable in his chair. I sat on the edge of the bed, opened my rucksack and produced the book of World War One poetry. I opened it and showed him the picture of Noel Clark. 'Do you recognize him?' I asked. Billy stared hard at the grainy photo and frowned. 'Maybe you've heard some of his poems?' I went on. I read him 'Trench Winter' followed by 'Survivors'. 'Mean anything to you?' I asked when I'd finished. Billy's eyes were deep pools of blankness. 'OK,' I said. 'Just an idea. Not to worry, eh.' Feeling mildly exasperated, I got up. Sometimes talking to Billy was like cycling to Pluto. I replaced the book. 'I'm going now,' I said. 'See you next Sunday.'

I had my hand on the doorknob when Billy suddenly gave a deep sigh. I turned round instantly. 'What?' I said crossing to him. 'Are you OK?' Billy worked his mouth a bit. Then he gave up. His face crumpled, like a deflated balloon. 'Aw, Billy, it doesn't matter,' I said feeling terrible. He'd obviously tried to tell me something and failed. The poems must have stirred up old memories. Opened wounds. Then I had an idea. 'Can you draw it?' I suggested. I handed him his pad and box of crayons. Billy looked marginally more cheerful. He flipped open the pad, selected a pencil, thought for a second or two, then bent over the paper, a frown of concentration deepening between his brows.

I watched with rising excitement as Billy began to draw. This could be a breakthrough, I thought. Perhaps I was on the brink of discovering something. Billy's fingers fumbled awkwardly with the pencils. 'Keep going,' I encouraged him. I peered over his shoulder as the drawing began to take shape:

a man lying on the ground with a wound in his head. A group of soldiers standing a little way off, ignoring him. With a sinking feeling of déjà-vu, I recognized what he was drawing. It was what he always drew. Billy's favourite battle scene. Mrs Morrison had a version of it in her office. There was one in the kitchen, a framed one in the residents' lounge. For some reason, he seemed reluctant to draw anything else. I could barely contain my disappointment.

Billy finished the sketch. Then he tore it out of the book and handed it to me. I tried to sound grateful. 'Yeah, Billy, that's nice. Thanks,' I said, but in reality I was bitterly disappointed. I'd hoped for some sort of revelation. I tucked the drawing into my pocket, watered his hyacinth, which was already in bud, and went home.

Time is a head thing. A minute can pass quickly or take so long, roots grow in your brain. For Billy, time had stopped moving altogether; his roots were now forever embedded in the past, feeding on memories deeply buried somewhere inside his silence. Now, it was all too long ago and too far away for him to make sense of it. I felt guilty for upsetting him. I knew, for a flickering instant, I had disturbed something. I had heard it, seen it in his face. A tantalizing glimpse into a hidden world. But there was no way to break through the barrier.

On Monday I went for my second workout and came back inspired again. Once more, I resolved to lay off fattening food and major on fruit and salad. Unfortunately, it was December, it was cold, and my brain kept redirecting me to the kitchen. Norwegians like to eat in the winter, it's their temperament. And I'm no different—they can take me out of Norway, but they can't take Norway out of me! I held off for two days, then gave in and hit the chocolate. Will-power is a head thing too.

On Wednesday, I went into town with my mother to watch the Christmas lights being switched on. It's always done by some tacky soap star but I like to see it. The beginning of Christmas for real. This Christmas, I'd decided to give my room a complete makeover. I'd bought a book on *feng shui* and was already working out how I'd arrange everything. Woodblock flooring and a futon were essential to my plans, so I'd started creeping stealthily down the hint trail.

And Grant? I hadn't forgotten my investigation. Every afternoon, I rang Jimmy's but there was never any reply. By Friday, I was fed up. Jimmy's was my only lead and I really didn't want to go trekking across town again. It was cold and I had too much to do. I decided I'd give it until the end of term. Two weeks. If I hadn't had some sort of breakthrough by then, I'd stop. It was only fair. After all, I'd done everything I could, asked all the right people. I'd come up with nothing but dead ends. Perhaps I just wasn't meant to find out who killed Grant. Or perhaps I was losing interest. Other things were starting to replace him. It was as if I'd enjoyed getting in touch with my Inner Detective but maybe we were on the verge of parting company.

On Sunday, I went to visit Billy again. This time, however, I didn't take the poems with me, I took a box of Milk Tray instead. I like edible apologies. Billy and I munched our way steadily through the chocs whilst I told him about my exams but I sensed he wasn't listening. I knew the signs, I'd been in enough boring lessons. Then he started dozing off in his chair. So I didn't stay long. I left him to his memories.

I'd barely got used to waking up without that sinking feeling that meant school when it was time to go back. Study leave had flown by so swiftly. The time thing again. I wasn't looking forward to Monday. Mentally joining up the dots of that last week at school, I kept hearing Lee's mocking voice, seeing Helen's piggy little eyes glaring at me. Feeling the corporate hostility. Compared to them, exams were a minor blip on my horizon.

I remember every detail of that Monday. A cold day, the smell of rain in the air. First day of the exams: English, Paper 1, and History. I had a good breakfast—muesli, syrup waffles, and a glass of grapefruit juice. Checked I had spare cartridges in my pencil case and Hakon my lucky troll.

We registered quickly, then went straight to the gym. Nobody gave me any hassle, everybody was too preoccupied, nervous. We had to sit in long alphabetical rows, to prepare us for the real exams in the summer. Like greyhounds waiting for the off, we sat straining at our mental leashes, watching the hands of the big clock creeping towards 9.30. Warnings were given about speaking or making eye contact so everyone stared straight ahead. You could cut the tension with a knife. At last we were told: 'You may open your paper and begin.' I wished myself '*lykke til!*', turned over my exam paper and tried not to panic as my mind went totally blank.

I don't recall any of the questions. I remember I was still writing when the order came to finish. In silence, we packed up and filed out of the gym. Most people went to the toilets for a group panic. I went to the canteen for an early lunch (chips, sausages, and baked beans). Then straight to the library to cram for the afternoon.

At 3.30, we finished the History exam. I was exhausted—I'd been writing for four hours with only an hour's break in between. My fingers felt numb, my wrist ached, and I had a sore left elbow from leaning it on my desk. I exchanged rueful glances with the girl at the next table. She was suffering too. Outside the gym, I chatted to some people I knew—we discussed how hard the questions were, how badly we'd done, and how we'd not opened a book all week. The usual lies you always tell after an exam. I spotted Helen, Tracie, and Lee with a group from my form, but I carefully avoided them. As I left the PE block and went to get my stuff from my locker, I heard a voice behind me. 'Hey, Viking, wait up.' I turned my head. It was Lee. I instantly quickened my pace. 'Viking—wait!' I broke into a jog. Lee came alongside me. 'Hey, Viking, slow down.' I started running.

'Sorry,' I said panting. 'Got things to do.'

We were on the threshold of B block. Lee put on an extra spurt and reached the door a fraction of a second before me. He stood across it, barring my way.

'Oh no,' he said grimly, 'you don't get away so easily.'

I skidded to an unsteady halt. 'What's this all about?' I gasped, fighting for breath.

'Kelly,' Lee said. 'I want to talk to you about Kelly.'

'Excuse me?'

'You know Kelly. She's a friend of Grant's. She went round his house the other week to get her science book back.'

'So? Look, first I don't know what you're talking about and second, I have to get my stuff,' I puffed.

'Not until you tell me about Kelly.' Lee folded his arms.

'Like I said, Kelly who?' I snapped. I wasn't going to admit anything to him.

'Exactly. Kelly who,' Lee exclaimed triumphantly. 'Grant didn't have any friends called Kelly.'

'And you'd know? Maybe he did but he just didn't tell you.' I glared angrily at Lee. He was bugging the shit out of me! I'd just done four hours of exams. I was tired. I wanted to go home, relax. How dare he waylay me, try to stop me getting my things? I decided to get nasty. Play dirty. 'Actually, come to think of it, Grant didn't tell you a whole lot, did he?' I sneered. 'After all, you didn't know he was doing porn.' Lee winced; I'd hit home. 'Yeah,' I went on, determined to twist the knife. 'Like you were such good mates—not. He didn't even try to get a message to you before he died, did he?'

For a moment, Lee looked so mad, I thought he was going to hit me. Then suddenly, his expression changed. His mouth fell open. He swore loudly. 'His out-box,' he exclaimed. 'Christ—nobody checked his out-box.'

'Excuse me?'

'Of course. That's it! Geez, I'm so bloody stupid!'

'Huh?'

Lee leaped away from the door. 'Sorry,' he yelled over his shoulder. 'Speak to you later. Got to go!' He ran off towards the cycle shed. I stared after him in astonishment. Bloody nutter! I hadn't a clue what he was talking about. Still, it was no concern of mine. At least I was free to get my stuff now.

Mr Richards was in the form room, marking books. He looked up and smiled as I came in. 'So, Annie, how was the exam?'

'Terrible, sir,' I sighed and shook my head. 'Really hard.'

You have to say things like that. For some reason, teachers like to think they're making your life difficult. I don't know why. Anyway, Mr Richards looked pleased, so I felt I'd accomplished my mission: I'd made his life happy. I got my things and went home. I felt shattered. And puzzled. What on earth was Lee playing at? I had a bath and made myself a huge bowl of fruit salad. Just as well it was Art the next day. No revision. All I had to do was pack my Discman and enough CDs to keep me going for five hours.

I wasn't going to go to my exercise class at first. Too tired. Then I changed my mind—if I couldn't run from the PE block to B block without feeling I'd climbed Mount Everest, I reasoned, I must still be pretty unfit. I needed exercise. So, rather reluctantly I uncurled myself from the sofa, got dressed in my tracksuit and went. It had started to rain; the roads were wet and shiny. I weaved in and out of the traffic, wishing I'd stayed at home after all. However, once the class had started, the adrenalin kicked in and I began to feel good, glad I'd made the effort.

The night was silver with rain when I came out. I pulled my jacket hood over my head and went to get my bike. But when I took it from the rack, I discovered that I'd got a flat back tyre. I cursed myself—I must have gone over some glass in the road. It was a very long walk home. I decided to go back and see if I could ring my mother. I was just heading for the pay-phone when somebody called to me. 'Hello—Annie, isn't it?' I turned in the direction of the voice and recognized Jimmy—the owner of the boxing club where Grant had gone. He was wearing chinos and a dark blue shirt. Very nice. He came straight over to me, smiling like I was a long-lost friend. I felt myself blushing. 'Well, this is a coincidence,' he said. 'We meet again.'

'Yeah—I've been trying to ring you,' I mumbled, wishing I'd washed my hair and bothered to put on a bit of make-up. Still, he'd remembered my name! I was flattered. There were teachers in my school who'd taught me for years and didn't know who I was. Seeing him again, I felt my interest in Grant being rekindled. Maybe I was on the verge of the break I'd been hoping for.

'I wanted to talk to you about those classes you promised,' I said. 'Only now I have to ring home—my bike's got a flat tyre.'

'Hey, bad luck,' Jimmy said sympathetically. 'You want a lift?'

'Er . . . ' I pulled a face. Years of indoctrination kicked in automatically.

'Don't worry—you're safe with me,' Jimmy smiled, noticing my hesitation. 'Hey, Stacey, come and tell Annie who I am, will you. She thinks I'm going to kidnap her.'

Stacey, my class leader, was standing chatting to a friend. She looked up and came over.

'Hi, Mr Whitehouse,' she said politely.

'You see?' Jimmy grinned at me. 'Stacey here will vouch for me. She knows who pays her wages.' Stacey gave a rather forced smile.

Mr Whitehouse? 'You own this place?' I stuttered. Jimmy nodded. 'But I thought you owned that other place,' I said.

'Own them both, Annie,' Jimmy said. 'Jimmy's—that's for the boxing fraternity. This place—different clientele. Bit more up-market. You tried it yet?'

'Annie comes to my class,' Stacey put in.

'Hey—good for you, Annie!' Jimmy exclaimed enthusiastically. 'That's what I like to hear. So . . . what about that lift? We can put your bike in the boot and talk about those classes you wanted on the way.'

This time I didn't hesitate. 'OK.' I nodded. I followed Jimmy happily out to the car park. This was great. I had a lift and the chance to do a bit more investigation. Things were going my way.

Jimmy's car was a brand new black top-of-the-range BMW. Very very nice. He must be absolutely loaded, I thought, as I lifted my bike into the boot and then slid into the smooth leather upholstered front seat. I gave him directions and then sat back to enjoy the ride.

I could get used to this, I thought, as the car purred smoothly and silently out of the car park. I watched the hypnotic arcing of the windscreen wipers and felt glad I was the other side to them. It was a foul night.

'So, Annie,' Jimmy said, 'will you get your dad or brother to fix the bike for you?'

I grimaced. I hate it when people assume I'm not capable of doing some basically simple mechanical job.

'I shall do it myself,' I replied sharply. 'I'm not stupid.'

'Whoa—no offence.' Jimmy laughed. I noticed he wore big gold rings on both hands and a gold Rolex on his left wrist. Rich man's jewellery. And he smelled of expensive cologne. We drove on in silence for a bit. Then Jimmy said casually, 'I don't suppose you fancy earning a bit of extra cash, do you?'

'Sorry?'

'Well, I was thinking, I was planning to do some publicity for the centre—posters, maybe a promotional video. I could use somebody like you.'

'Me?' I was amazed.

'Yeah—you're just what I'm looking for, a strong-minded independent young lady.'

'Well,' I hesitated. 'I don't know.'

'It's good money,' Jimmy said, staring out of the window at the traffic. 'Look, no pressure. Why don't you take one of my cards—go on, help yourself—in the dashboard. They've got my personal number on. Have a think and phone me if you're interested.'

I hesitated. I couldn't really see myself on a poster. Unless it was for weight-watchers. Before rather than after. But I didn't want to offend him. After all, he was giving me a lift. And I wanted to find out more about Grant. So I reached forward obediently and took a card from the compartment.

'Great,' Jimmy said. He turned and smiled at me. It felt good when he did that, like it did when I said something intelligent in class. I slipped the card into my pocket.

'Left here,' I directed him. We turned the corner. The car came up behind a boy on a bike. Even through the rain-spattered windscreen I recognized him as one of the Year Ten's from my school. He was weaving around the puddles.

Jimmy swore. 'Bloody cyclist! He's all over the road!' He hooted a couple of times. The boy swerved into the kerb. The car passed very close to him, drenching him with water. Angrily, the boy raised two fingers. I waved at him out of the back window as we sped off. And suddenly, I froze, my hand halfway in the air. My mind flashed back to another rainy night. A lone cyclist and a car that passed too close. A black car that hooted in exactly the same way. I remembered a passenger, vaguely familiar, in the front of that car, who had waved as it sped away. And the last piece of jigsaw dropped neatly and silently into place. All at once I knew the identity of that passenger—it was Grant Penney. And the car that had passed on that rainy night was the one I was sitting in right now. Lee had got it wrong: the last person to see Grant alive was me. Then I recalled Jimmy telling me that he'd not seen Grant for months because he'd been out of the country. He had lied to me. Why? Suddenly, I realized there was only one possible answer to that question. My heart jumped and I felt a cold shiver go down my spine.

I do not know how I managed to survive the rest of that journey. My throat was dry. My heart pounded so loudly that I was surprised he didn't hear it. My hands were clenched so tightly together that afterwards I could trace the imprint of my nails on each palm. I had to force my mouth shut—all I wanted to do was scream and scream. At last, after what seemed like hours, we reached the top of my road. I leaped out as if escaping from fire. Then I had to wait those agonizing last few minutes while he opened the boot, got my bike out for me. I had to act grateful, say thanks, yes I'd consider his offer, no I hadn't time to fix up a meeting, sorry, not now, I had to get home—exam tomorrow, I'd be in touch, bye and thanks again.

I ran all the way home, pushing my useless bike. I fixed the puncture. Then I went straight to the police. I didn't think they'd believe me. But to my surprise, they took it very seriously. What I didn't know was that what I told them merely confirmed what they already knew. A few hours earlier, they'd had another visitor: Lee Scott. He supplied them with proof of what I said. The truth, the whole truth, written by somebody who knew exactly what had happened to Grant Penney on that fateful day.

Lee and Grant were computer addicts. They liked to surf the Net—check out sport sites, play games. They e-mailed each other. Swapped interesting Web addresses. The irony was, Lee told me later, he'd actually e-mailed Grant the night he died. Got no reply. Thought nothing more about it till the news of Grant's suicide broke. He'd gone round to the house, asked if Grant had left a message on his computer. Grant's mum said no, nothing. Lee believed her. It was only when we'd talked earlier that day that something clicked in his brain and he suddenly realized Grant might just have left a message in his outbox but failed to send it. And his mum wouldn't know because by the time she got in, the only thing on the screen would have been the screen saver. Grant's mum knew nothing about computers; she'd have turned it off without checking. So Lee went and checked. And it was there. Grant's suicide note. The letter nobody had found because they'd all looked in the wrong place.

`sorry about tonite,` **(Grant wrote)** `couldn't get it together, must be losing my magic. losing something is right, anyway, i want to tell you about whats been going on, like you said, yeah things have changed and you were right, like always. only you got one thing wrong, it's me thats changed not you. so this is where i explain it all, or try to.`

`you remember last term how i got that notice off the board at school—the boxing club. you remember i told you about jimmy, the boss, how he was really cool, well he's the reason for it all. first off it was ok there. i was learning stuff, I got good with the gloves, could fight guys older than me and win every time. they said i was a natural, i felt great. it was like i was getting respect from everybody. so jimmy comes up to me one day and asks me to do some promo shots for the club. i was really blown away, so of course i said yes, so we went to this studio he has at the back of his house, really professional, like a real photographers, cameras on tripods` and different lighting and a dark room as well and he took these shots with me shadow boxing and stuff. i thought when these come out, it's going to be well wicked, all the girls will fancy me. i thought at last i'm going to be a babe-magnet. i wanted you to be jealous—you're the one who always pulls. i was so stupid. he gave me money too. a lot of money. that was when i got my leather jacket, remember. you said where did i get the cash, i wouldn't tell you and we had that big row. i'm sorry, i should have told you then, before it got heavy but i wanted to be like you, i was so stupid, lee. i'm sorry.

so after a bit, jimmy asks me to do some more shots, because the other ones hadn't come out the way he wanted. he said he'd pay me again so of course i said yes. this time it was after the club closed, he got me on the fitness equipment and we did a couple more sessions, me using the rowing machine, stuff like that. he paid well so i didn't see anything wrong with it, bit of a laugh really that's all it was.

next thing i know, jimmy says he's shown the prints to a mate of his and he wants me to do some modelling for him. i really thought i was on the edge of a career break, going to give the school two fingers. i thought i'd show all of them. i wanted to see the look on old ritchy's face when i told him. i'd say sucker, i'll be earning a small fortune any time now, i don't need you. i'm sorry mate. i was so stupid but its too late now.

so after school jimmy picked me up and took me to his friend's place out of town and that's where it all started to go wrong. i didn't want to do the stuff they asked but jimmy kept telling me it was ok, lots of real models do shots like that all the time, he said. so i did it but i wasn't happy. the money was good though. too good. i should of stopped then but i'd got used to having money, it was like a drug. i never had much now i had it to burn, spent it as fast as i got it on the bike and the computer and other stuff, i told mum i was working down the club when she asked where i got it from. i wasn't happy about the pictures they took, but i thought maybe after a bit i'd say no more photos. only i made a mistake about that one, didn't i, because next jimmy comes back and says they want to make a film because he said there were guys abroad who'd pay good money for it. well, i knew what sort of film he meant.

so now it wasn't a laugh any more, but when i said no, he got really angry. he said i must of known where this was going, he said i couldn't back out now he'd got everything set up. he said he'd done so much for me, i couldn't let him down, i owed him big time. then he said if i didn't agree he'd send the pictures to mum and the school. i was so scared. he kept on and on, putting on the pressure. i knew he was serious. i didn't know what to do. i was so scared and there was nobody i could talk to.

that was when i started bunking off all the time. it was because he waited outside the gate.

somedays he'd follow me home. it was like he was a different person. you know how people get you in their power, it was like that. i hated him but i couldn't stop him. i was so scared, lee, in the end i said i'd do it. anything to get him off my back, stop the pressure. it was like a pain that wouldn't go away. i was thinking about it all the time. what he wanted me to do. what would happen if i said no.

it was going to be after school today. he picked me up in his car but i couldn't go through with it. i jumped out at the lights and ran home. he's going to do something bad now, i know it, i saw it in his eyes when i jumped out. it's doing my head in. i can't think straight anymore. he's got my bike. i don't know what to tell mum. i've been sitting here for hours but i can't think straight. it's all gone wrong for me. i made a terrible mistake and now there's only one way out.

i think i'm going to do it tonite. i thought about it a lot over the last few days. maybe a knife. i could make the blade cut through the layers of skin no sweat. easy. i'd be happy to see the blood running down. no more stress, no more pain. maybe i'll do it another way because i can't stand the pain any more. i've let everyone down. this is how i see myself. it's too late to go back now anyway. sorry, the reason i'm writing is to say sorry it has to be like this, but i can't change it now. can't be anymore. g

Lee never got the letter because in his despair and confusion, Grant forgot to press the 'send' button before he hanged himself.

I didn't discover all this until the exams had practically finished. Just as well. If I'd known how close I was to being sucked into the same web of evil, I would probably have freaked. I only knew what I'd told the police. So I sat my exams thinking that was an end to the story. And I avoided coming into contact with Lee. Which, looking back, was a bit strange. After all, I'd succeeded where he had failed. But I didn't feel like gloating. In fact, I didn't feel anything at all, not then. So it wasn't until the police arrested Jimmy for supplying pornographic material over the Internet that I heard Lee's story for the first time—we both had to go down to the police station after school in the last week of term, to make statements and to be debriefed.

I learned then that Jimmy was involved in a large and sinister paedophile network called Wonderland. I learned how he used his health club outlets (he had several in various towns) to attract young teenagers. He lured them in by offering free membership and the chance to try out state of the art fitness equipment. It was an irresistible combination. The police told us Jimmy had an unerring eye for the solitary kid, the easily influenced one, and the misfit whom nobody liked. He would target them, single them out and befriend them. The rest was easy. Before long, his charm and his money had them eating out of his hand. Later, if they refused to comply with his wishes, he had ways of making them or of making sure they stayed silent. Grant's was not the only suicide linked to his organization. The police suspected him, wanted an excuse to raid his premises, but had no proof. Until we turned up. The teenage cavalry riding to the rescue.

We both made full statements. The detective in charge of

the case told us we probably wouldn't have to appear in court. Our statements were enough. I was relieved. I didn't want my name splashed all over the papers. A celebrity. Not for this.

After we'd finished our statements, we left the police station. I felt numb. I guess I was in shock. Everything had happened so quickly. We stood on the steps outside. There were still things that didn't make sense. I asked Lee where on earth he thought Grant had got the money from. Lee said Grant had told him about the modelling, but hadn't gone into details.

'And you believed him?' I exclaimed.

Lee said, 'It was a bit of a joke—I mean Grant wasn't exactly your model type. I asked him to put in a word for me,' he continued, 'but he never did. I didn't understand why. We had a row about it once.' Lee laughed bitterly. 'I called him selfish. Keeping all that money for himself.'

'Maybe he was protecting you,' I said.

'Yeah, I understand that now,' he said quietly.

Just before we split, Lee turned to me and said, 'Thank God it's all over.'

But it wasn't over for me. In the days that followed, I realized I would never be the same again. Something inside me had been destroyed. Briefly, evil had touched my life and taken a part of my childhood. The world would never feel entirely safe again.

■ 'Dulce et decorum est pro patria mori'

We always spend Christmas with my mother's parents. They live in York. Every year I made a big fuss about going, but I enjoy it once I get there. York is a great city. You can feel history in the streets. I specially like the Viking centre. It's good to remind myself I come from a long line of conquering warriors.

We were going to drive up to York on Wednesday, which only gave me a couple of days to buy presents. I don't buy much for my grandparents—chocolate, bath stuff. My parents used to send them a photo of me each Christmas. That was when we lived in Norway. Not now. Now they get to see the real thing even if it is only once a year. Much better. Anyway I hate having my photo taken—my cute factor is in the minus zone.

We broke up Friday lunchtime. As soon as the bell went, I was out of that door like a mole on a motorbike. No hanging around. There was nobody I wanted to wish '*god jul*'. I hadn't written any cards, though I got a few. One from Lee, which was a surprise. Since the visit to the police, we'd barely spoken.

I went into town and celebrated my freedom with a hamburger and fries at the Blue Dog. I had all the trimmings, cheese, bacon, onions, coleslaw on the side. Then some cheesecake and a lemon tea. Afterwards, I went to Boots and to Thorntons, the chocolate shop, and bought my presents. Then to the art shop for Billy's present—a box of Caran d'ache crayons. Normally, I enjoy buying presents. Now, I went about it feeling detached, emotionless. No pleasure whatsoever. Like I was watching myself from inside my head.

When I'd finished my shopping, I did something I'd been waiting to do for days. I cycled back to the White House Fitness Centre. Ever since they'd arrested Jimmy, I'd been secretly scared that I'd be tracked down by an accomplice. So I went and cancelled my membership. I stood and actually watched the receptionist wipe my details from the computer files. Suddenly, I ceased to exist. It was a huge relief. Now I could stop looking over my shoulder. I could start to feel safe.

I returned home to wrap my presents.

On Sunday, I went to give Billy his gift. All days were the same to him, so I reckoned it wouldn't matter if it was a week early. Christmas had broken out all over Elmfield. There was a red poinsettia on the reception desk and a brightly decorated Christmas tree in one corner. An even bigger tree adorned the residents' lounge. It was all covered with tinsel, twinkly lights, and fake snow. A small plastic Santa and sleigh perched precariously on top of the TV. Every picture was awash with tinsel and there were banners on the walls with cheesy greetings like: 'Christmas is "snow" fun without you'. I could imagine Christmas Day: the oldies sitting down to a slap-up Christmas lunch, cooked by Mr Reeve, paper hats wobbling on their heads, before falling asleep in front of the Queen's speech. As I made my way down the paper-chain hung corridor, I almost wished I could spend Christmas with them. It'd be more fun than sitting around making polite conversation with rellies I don't see from one year to the next. Particularly this Christmas. I didn't feel like playing happy families. I'd rather be busy. It kept my mind from thinking. Give me a sink full of washing up, I thought, and unlimited access to the leftovers. I'd be content.

Billy was sitting in his chair, wrapped in his rug.

'Hi, Billy,' I greeted him. 'Merry Christmas.' I bent and placed the parcel in his lap. Then I stood and watched his fingers awkwardly fumbling the brightly coloured wrapping. I wondered when he'd last had a present. He seemed to remember what to do, even though it took ages to accomplish. Finally, he worked his way to the box and opened the lid.

'Do you like them?' I said. Billy stared. He picked each crayon up and examined it closely. 'They're for your drawings,' I told him. 'Happy Christmas.' Billy looked at me. Then, suddenly, his face wrinkled up and he smiled. I'd never seen him smile before. It added a couple of hundred wrinkles to his face. 'Hey, you like them!' I said softly. I handed him his old wooden box so that he could transfer the new crayons into it, but to my surprise, Billy tipped the contents into the new box, filling it to the top. He thrust the old box into my hands. 'You don't want it?' I asked. He shook his head. 'OK, I'll bin it.' Billy made inarticulate noises. 'What?' I said. Billy folded his hands round mine, pushing the box towards me. His eyes peered at me. I could see the muscles in his wrinkled throat moving convulsively as he tried to form words. 'You want me to have the box?' I asked. Billy nodded, keeping his papery-skinned hands round mine. 'Christmas present?' Billy nodded again. 'OK,' I slipped the box into my shoulder bag. 'It's a nice present. Thanks.'

I settled him more comfortably in his chair, the box of crayons and his sketch pad on his lap. Silence descended. Billy drew, breathing noisily. I stared out of the window, allowing my mind to drift. What still terrified me even now, I thought, was how close I'd got to slipping into Jimmy Whitehouse's power. He had been so nice, so plausible, that I'd believed him, liked him. Almost fancied him. Over and over, I tortured myself by speculating what might have happened to me had I agreed to do that fake photo shoot. It didn't bear thinking about.

And there was something else that bothered me. In discovering who had killed Grant, I'd also uncovered a link between us. Something we had in common. I think that really disturbed me the most because I'd always hated Grant. In my eyes he belonged to a lower species of humanity. Somewhere between Neanderthal man and ape. I considered myself vastly superior to him in every respect. So it came as a shock to discover that we were both on Jimmy's wish list. The kids he targeted for his special attention. The select few. Grant Penney and me: misfit and loner. That was really scary.

I was awakened from my reverie by a crash. The box had fallen from Billy's lap, spilling crayons all over the floor. I sighed. Back to reality. I got down on my hands and knees and collected the crayons, replacing them in the box. Billy's eyes were closed. He must have fallen asleep. I was slightly surprised the noise had not wakened him. I sat back on my heels and looked up into his face. It was serene and peaceful and suddenly I knew what had happened and why he had not stirred. Billy would never wake again.

I left the box on the floor and returned to my chair. I felt no sorrow. No more war for him, I thought, nor any suffering. No life lived in shadows. The sweet smell of hyacinth filled the room. White hyacinth, the colour of peace. I watched as the afternoon faded slowly into evening and the shades of death gently smoothed the lines on Billy's face. Finally, I got up and tiptoed over to him. He looked so tranquil. I bent down and kissed his cheek. '*Adjo da, bestefar*,' I whispered softly, 'God speed your journey.'

Then I went to find Mrs Morrison.

We returned from York early so that I could go to the funeral. The church was full. Everyone came to say farewell to Billy Donne. People who'd never known him, like the mayor and the local press—only there to be seen and to take photos. And those people who'd known him and cared for him: the staff and residents of Elmfield. I had never been to an English funeral before. I listened to the words and thought how beautiful they were. Mrs Morrison had asked me to say something in the service about what Billy meant to me. I knew I could not put my feelings into words so I read Noel Clark's poem 'Survivors', my voice echoing strangely round the church. Afterwards, Mr Reeve came over and shook my hand and Mrs Jones hugged me. Mrs Morrison told me to stay in touch, but I knew in my heart I wouldn't. Billy had been the connection between us. There was nothing at Elmfield for me now he was dead.

It might have ended there. Standing at Billy's graveside on a bitterly cold December afternoon. I threw a handful of earth into the grave. The past was buried. I let it go. I would never forget, but I had my life to get on with. The jigsaw was complete; time to close the box. Over the next few days, I thought about my future, made plans. I decided to create harmony, balance, and a sense of space in my bedroom. My mother told me she couldn't afford woodblock flooring and a futon, so I hired a sander and stripped and varnished the floorboards myself. We visited her work friends to see the New Year in and I drank too much beer. Then it was time to get ready for school again.

On the Sunday morning before my first day back, I dug my bag out from under a pile of junk. I opened it and threw my textbooks in. There was a splintering sound. For a moment, I was puzzled. Then I remembered Billy's box. Hot damn! I peered into the bag. Textbooks and shards of old wood everywhere. I removed the wood and binned it. Sad. Thanks to my carelessness, my last link with Billy Donne had gone for ever.

I didn't find the notebook until later that evening. I was finishing off some last minute work that I'd promised myself I'd do before Christmas. I started groping around in the bottom of the bag for some chocolate I thought I remembered leaving in it. My fingers folded around something soft and oblong. Chocolate shaped but not chocolate. I pulled it out of my bag. A shabby little brown book, the corners frayed and torn. Not mine, I thought. So whose? I flicked the book open, started reading the slanting old-fashioned writing.

I write this down as a true account of what happened on April 8th 1917. I was there. I know what I saw. This is my account of what happened on that day. If those in authority wish to deny it, they can, but every detail is engraved upon my mind as clear as day and I will testify before God and in any court of law in the land that what I write is true.

We marched into Arras on April 2nd. Our regiment was to join the Third Army, under General Allenby. Our mission was to attack the Hindenburg Line and advance to Cambrai. The town was a mess, all ruined buildings and burned out shops, but as we passed through, there was a military band playing in the Grand Place and we stopped to listen. On the outskirts of the town, I saw railway trucks loaded with earth from the trenches and tunnels that were being excavated in preparation for the battle.

In the grey dawn, we marched up the line to the trenches and I remembered marching up the line to my first ever battle. We were all green and innocent! Biff the Boche, be home for Christmas—it was like a kid's game. I was seventeen and I'd lied my way into the army. We sang as we marched then. No singing this time, just the sound of weary boots trudging along the rutted road. How old am I now? I have lost count of how many battles, how many feet of ground I've fought across. How many stinking water-logged trenches I've cowered in. Which was the trench with the dead Boche in its wall? I forget. We used to hang our kitbags on his putrefying arm as it stuck out from the sandbagged wall. I have seen such horrific things.

When we got back to the trenches, we were told by our lieutenant that we'd be joined by some soldiers from another regiment. They'd lost a lot of their officers and two-thirds of their men and had been ordered to combine with our group. Poor sods, I thought. No respite for them then.

We made camp in a nice dry cave and settled down for a rest and a brew. After a bit, the other soldiers arrived. They were in bad shape. One man in particular was really bad, white-faced, mad eyes, shaking like a leaf. I offered him a mug of tea but his hands were shaking so much he couldn't hold it. I've seen a lot of men like that. It's the noise of the guns and the thought that maybe there's a bullet with your name on it. Makes you go barmy in the head. Shell shock, they call it. On the first day of the Somme, I lost all my mates in the first few seconds. I wake up in the night and see their faces.

The night of the 7th was very cold, snow in the air. We knew the next morning at dawn we'd go up to the forward trenches ready for the attack. Everybody was quiet, thinking about the coming battle. Some of the men wrote home. I used to write but I don't any more. Not since my letter was returned with 'not known at this address' written on it. I knew then that she had not waited for me to come back. Now there is nobody to write to.

The man I'd noticed earlier on was very down. He sat apart from the rest of us, staring at the ground. I went over and tried to cheer him up. 'Don't worry, mate,' I said, 'chances are, we'll all live to fight another day.' He just looked at me with wild haunted eyes. I remember I thought: Christ, I wouldn't like to be thinking what you're thinking. I asked him his name but he didn't reply. I wasn't offended. Sometimes I wake up and can't remember my name either. One thing surprised me though, when I saw him shuffle into the cave, shoulders bent almost double and grey-faced with tiredness, I thought he was quite old. Now I realized with a shock that he was only young.

Around midnight, I must have dozed off into an uneasy sleep. I woke up suddenly in the early dawn, my heart racing, thinking I heard the sound of gunfire in the distance somewhere. I didn't go back to sleep after that but sat watching the pale dawn creeping slowly into the cave. A bit later, the officer came in and ordered us all to get on our feet and line up outside. We stumbled into the cold sunlight. I looked around and did a quick count of heads. At first I thought we were all present and correct. Then I realized that the young man was missing. I thought he must have stepped out to obey a call of nature. I hoped he would return soon, the officers here are sticklers for discipline.

We were marched a little way to a level piece of terrain. That was when we saw the missing man. He was lying on the ground, blood streaming from his head. He was writhing in agony and crying out. A couple of us rushed forward but we were pushed back roughly by the officers. 'Leave the bugger alone,' one said. 'He's a mucking coward. Tried to take the easy way out.'

Then I understood: the poor man had shot himself. That must have been the sound that wakened me.

What happened next is something I will never forget, no, not if I live to be a hundred. The officers (whose names I know though I won't write them here) ordered us to stand and watch him die. To teach us a lesson, in case any of us wanted to follow his example. It was terrible. Every second of that young man's anguish is seared upon my brain. I can still hear the groans and strange animal noises he made as his life ebbed away. His eyes were open the whole time though he did not appear to recognize anything. From time to time he cried out for someone to help him. The officers would not give him any morphia to ease his pain. It took him three hours to die.

The man's name was Noel Clark. His rank was Private. One of his pals said he was a bit of a poet.

I feel I must write it all down as it preys upon my mind so much. I think now that I should have done more to help him. I dream about him. I see him lying on the cold ground and I hear his groans. I see the officers standing around waiting for him to die. I shall always remember what happened. It will be etched on my mind for eternity. Maybe I should have stepped forward and put another bullet into him and ended his pain but I was afraid of what might happen to me, so I did nothing.

Tonight I am on sentry duty again. The moonlight is so bright that I can see every shell hole. The water in the bottom is like silver. Beautiful, until I look up and remember where I am.

I shall hide this little book somewhere safe where it cannot be found by those who would want to destroy it to save their stinking reputations. But at the end of this terrible war, if I survive, I will make sure the murdering bastards fry in hell for what they did.

Tomorrow we go over the top again. I am so tired that my bones ache. What a long war this is! The gunfire in my head keeps me awake at nights. I hope there is a bullet with my name on it waiting out there for me.

If this notebook should be found by somebody then it means I am no longer alive. If so, whoever you are, please ask God to forgive me if you can, and say a prayer for my soul and for his.

Corporal William Frederick Donne. April 20th 1917. Arras

The rest of the pages were blank. I closed the book, feeling as if I had come back from very far away and very long ago. I sat looking at my montage of poems and pictures until my eyes were blinded by tears. Then I knelt down, my heart in pieces, and said a prayer for Billy Donne and Noel Clark.

■ Sometimes you have to follow your fears to find your destiny

Returning to school was not difficult for me; it was impossible. My outlook on life, my priorities, had completely altered. Every day felt as if I was in a country whose rules, customs, and language were no longer familiar to me. I had nothing to say, no wish to be there. On the outside, I was still me. Inside, everything was in turmoil. As if, after being born nearly sixteen years ago, I was now giving birth to myself. Fortunately, the Easter term was a short one. I kept my head down and worked. The library became my solace. Three weeks after Easter, study leave began and I left. I came back only to sit my exams. I didn't even show up to the Leavers' Disco in July.

Just before Easter, Jimmy Whitehouse's trial took place in London. He was found guilty and imprisoned. It made the national press. No mention of the part played by me or Lee, thankfully. Whilst the trial was on, there were several marches by groups protesting about paedophiles. They carried banners demanding safety on the streets, chanted slogans about the rights of children. It was big news. We even had a Citizenship lesson on the danger of strangers. I wanted to speak out, to say that it was not strangers we had to fear. It was the so-called friend, the adult you looked up to, the role-model. But I kept silent.

In the end, I did surprisingly well in my GCSEs, given all that had happened. A lot of top grades. Good enough to get me into higher education. I had decided ages ago that I didn't want to study A levels—too narrow for what I planned to do with my life. So I chose the IB—the International Baccalaureate, which meant I had to go to college rather than stay on for the Sixth Form.

College was OK. It suited me. People treated me like an adult. I could come and go as I wanted. Pace myself work-wise. I liked it there. But I didn't entirely lose touch with school. A couple of months into my course, I accidentally ran into Lee Scott. He was doing Media Studies at college. Perhaps it was because we were on neutral territory, I don't know, but we started chatting. We got on all right. First time ever. College must have mellowed me. After that, we began meeting for lunch. One thing led to another and, unbelievably, we even went out together for a time. It didn't last though. Too many ghosts. He's going with Tracie now.

I took the final exams in June. Now I am waiting for my results. In September, all being well, I shall be going on a long journey: I am returning to Norway, to Tromsø—the northernmost university in the world—where I hope to study Earth Sciences. And one day I intend to make another journey, even further north this time. To the land of mountains and fjords and snow, where winter temperatures can drop to −50 degrees and the sun never sets from May to the end of July. I am going to find my father, to share with him what has happened in my life. I need to understand the questions that have no answers. To see how the unconnected connect. The butterfly and the tidal wave. Perhaps then I'll be able to find a place for the last bit of jigsaw—the piece with my face on it—and maybe there will be a happy ending.

Or are happy endings only for story books . . . ?